The Symphonies of Beethoven
Part II

Professor Robert Greenberg

THE TEACHING COMPANY ®

PUBLISHED BY:

THE TEACHING COMPANY
4840 Westfields Boulevard, Suite 500
Chantilly, Virginia 20151-2299
1-800-TEACH-12
Fax—703-378-3819
www.teach12.com

ISBN 1-56585-821-2

Robert Greenberg, Ph.D.

Chairman, Department of Music History and Literature
San Francisco Conservatory of Music

Robert Greenberg has composed over 40 works for a wide variety of instrumental and vocal ensembles. Recent performances of Greenberg's work have taken place in New York, San Francisco, Los Angeles, Chicago, England, Ireland, Italy, Greece, and The Netherlands, where his "Child's Play" for String Quartet was performed at the Concertgebouw of Amsterdam in 1993.

Dr. Greenberg holds degrees from Princeton University and the University of California at Berkeley, where he received a Ph.D. in music composition in 1984. His principal teachers were Edward Cone, Claudio Spies, Andrew Imbrie, and Olly Wilson. His awards include three Nicola De Lorenzo Prizes in composition, three Meet the Composer grants, and commissions from the Koussevitzky Foundation of the Library of Congress, the Alexander String Quartet, XTET, and the Dancer's Stage Ballet Company.

He is on the faculty of the San Francisco Conservatory of Music, where he is chair of the Department of Music History and Literature and director of curriculum of the Adult Extension Division. He is creator, host, and lecturer for the San Francisco Symphony's "Discovery Series."

He has taught and lectured extensively across North America and Europe, speaking to such corporations and musical institutions as the Van Cliburn Foundation, Arthur Andersen, Bechtel Investments, the Shaklee Corporation, the University of California/Haas School of Business Executive Seminar, the Association of California Symphony Orchestras, the Texas Association of Symphony Orchestras, and the Commonwealth Club of San Francisco.

His work as a teacher and lecturer has been profiled in the Wall Street Journal, Inc., magazine, and the San Francisco Chronicle. He is an artistic co-director and board member of COMPOSERS INC. His music is published by Fallen Leaf Press and CPP/Belwin and is recorded on the Innova label.

Dr. Greenberg lives with his wife Lori, daughter Rachel, and son Samuel in the Oakland, California hills.

Table of Contents

The Symphonies of Beethoven
Part II

The Symphonies of Beethoven

Scope:

There can be few people who have not heard Beethoven's name, the famous first four notes of his fifth symphony, or the first strains of his "Ode to Joy." Beethoven is one of the most revered composers in the history of Western music.

Why? He possessed a unique gift for communication. He radiated an absolute directness that makes his music totally accessible. The sheer emotional power of his music is readily understood. His revolutionary compositional ideas are not hard to appreciate.

Beethoven is widely recognized as one of the greatest of all symphonists—the composer who ripped apart the regimented formulas of classical symphonic style. His nine symphonies are the cornerstone of orchestral literature. The revolution that they represent influenced composers for the next hundred years and more. It was a revolution on every level: harmonic, melodic, rhythmic, formal, dramatic, self-expressive, and emotional. Beethoven led the charge to a totally new era. He booted out the restraint of 18th-century classicism and ushered in romantic self-expression. His symphonic offspring were the first statesmen of this new, musical democracy.

Beethoven's artistic progress is historically measured in three periods:

1. 1792–1802: Viennese period: This period is marked by his innovative treatment of classical style conventions. It includes the composition of Symphony Nos. 1 and 2.

2. 1803–'15: Heroic period: This period is marked by truly revolutionary breaks with classical style. It sees the composition of Symphonies Nos. 3, 4, 5, 6, 7 and 8.

3. 1820–'26: Late period: This period is dominated by the most revolutionary and influential composition of Beethoven's entire career: the Ninth Symphony. Here Beethoven fuses all art forms into one monumental work and heralds a new era of unfettered musical expression.

Over the course of these 32 lectures on the history and analysis of Beethoven's nine symphonies, we see how the composer revolutionized the classical concept of musical composition in his approach to form, rhythm, harmony, melody, drama, and self-expression. No one believed more fervently than did Beethoven that rules exist to be broken.

Lectures One through Four, entitled "Beethoven and the Heroic Style," introduce Beethoven the man and his musical development up to 1808. In order to put his musical achievements into perspective, we look at Beethoven's early life, his physical and spiritual development, and the historical circumstances and the prevailing musical style that influenced his development. We learn the basic tenets of the classical style and how Beethoven stretched those rules in his first two symphonies. We start to understand Beethoven as a man of his time, a man shaped by his emotional demons and physical ailments.

Lectures Five and Six, entitled "Symphony No. 1: Beethoven as Classicist, Tradition and Innovation" examine how Beethoven pushes the envelope in his very first symphony.

The next two lectures are entitled "Symphony No. 2: Beethoven at the Edge." Symphony No. 2 has an extraordinary expressive and compositional range that puts it at the outer edge of the classical style even as it approached Beethoven's new heroic aesthetic, which was fully realized in Symphony No. 3 of 1803. In 1796 Beethoven began to suffer a hearing loss. By 1802 it was apparent to him that his hearing disability was permanent. He expressed his terror in the Heiligenstadt Testament. Beethoven's hearing loss may be seen as the catalyst of the new compositional path upon which he then embarked, beginning with his second symphony. His physical and emotional struggle with his hearing disability broadened his character and reached into his compositional creativity.

Lectures Nine through Twelve, entitled "Symphony No. 3: The "New Path"—Heroism and Self-Expression," discuss Symphony No. 3 ("Eroica"), which marked Beethoven's coming of age. Upon it he built the whole of his subsequent output. It is the key work in Beethoven's musical revolution, a revolution precipitated by the crisis of his hearing problem. It is a metaphor for the eternal struggle of the hero against adversity, a struggle with which Beethoven personally identified.

Lectures Thirteen through Sixteen, entitled "Symphony No. 4: Consolidation of the New Aesthetic," discuss the chronology of Beethoven's Fourth, Fifth and Sixth symphonies and analyze the Fourth. This new aesthetic is seen as a modest but not major return to a more classical structure. Its traditional framework is filled with iconoclastic rhythms and harmonies that clearly mark it as a product of the composer's post-"Eroica" period.

Lectures Seventeen through Nineteen, entitled "Symphony No. 5: The Expressive Ideal Fully Formed," analyze the iconoclastic Fifth Symphony and explain how it crystallizes Beethoven's mature compositional innovations. He subjects form to context. He establishes motivic development as a fundamental of his art. He introduces the concept of drama into the formal layout of movements. He introduces the concept of rhythm as a narrative element and he decrees that music must, above all, be self-expression.

Lectures Twenty through Twenty-two, entitled "Symphony No. 6: The Symphony as Program," examine Beethoven's Sixth Symphony and its relationship to his love of nature. In this symphony, Beethoven elevates program music to a genre of substance.

Lectures Twenty-three and Twenty-four, entitled "Symphony No. 7: The Symphony as Dance," analyze Beethoven's kinetic and dance-inspired Seventh Symphony with references to major events of the period. He broke off his affair with his "immortal beloved" in 1812, with all the grief that that entailed. His hearing also took a precipitous downturn. Yet, and perhaps because of these personal disasters, he was able to write the exuberant Seventh Symphony. Moreover, this period saw a revival of Beethoven's fame and fortune. It was precipitated by the (unmerited) popularity of his battle symphony, "Wellington's Victory." This work was inspired by Wellington's defeat of Napoleon in Spain and premiered at the same concert as Beethoven's Seventh Symphony.

Lectures Twenty-five through Twenty-seven, entitled "Symphony No. 8: Homage to Classicism," analyze Beethoven's Eighth Symphony. We learn the answer to an age-old riddle: his "immortal beloved" was Antonie Brentano. We see how he was beside himself with grief and despair as a result of breaking off this affair. Yet he composed his exuberant battle symphony, "Wellington's Victory," and the Seventh Symphony, which brought him a temporary revival of public popularity in 1814. The Eighth symphony, full of raucous humor and brilliant wit, was born amidst these events and premiered in February 1814.

Lectures Twenty-eight through Thirty-two, entitled "Symphony No. 9: The Symphony as the World," analyze the Ninth Symphony and discuss the years surrounding the Ninth Symphony's genesis. We learn about Beethoven's fall from public favor in 1815; the loss of his most loyal patrons; his worsening hearing loss; his disastrous possessiveness toward his nephew Karl; the years of litigation to claim custody of Karl (1815–'20); his consequent emotional decline; and finally his rebirth with the composition of his late period works (1820–'26). We see how the Ninth Symphony obliterated time-honored distinctions in its conception as a *Gesamtkunstwerk*, a work that embraces all art forms, including literature, song, and drama. By its example, the ninth decreed that context dictates genre as well as form and that the expressive needs of the composer must take precedence over any and all musical conventions.

Lectures Nine–Twelve
Symphony No. 3—The "New Path"—
Heroism and Self-Expression, I-IV

Scope:

Lectures Nine through Twelve focus on Symphony No. 3, known as the "Eroica" Symphony. This is the key work in Beethoven's compositional revolution, which was, brought about by the psychological crisis of 1802 when the composer realized that he was going deaf. Beethoven's struggle to come to terms with his disability seems to have raised him to a new level of creativity. His personal crisis served as a catalyst for the "new path" that he would forge in his development as a composer. Symphony No. 3 parallels Beethoven's own life in its heroic battle with and ultimate triumph over adversity. The symphony's historical debt to Napoleon Bonaparte and the myth of Prometheus is discussed before we proceed to an in-depth analysis of the symphony.

Outline

I.   Introduction.

   A. Beethoven composed the bulk of his third symphony in 1803.

   B. The third symphony is the key work in Beethoven's musical revolution, a revolution brought about by the crisis that was precipitated by his seemingly incurable hearing problem.

   C. Gestation of Symphony No. 3: what we know and do not know.

   1. We know that Beethoven had ambivalent feelings about Napoleon.

   2. We know that in 1803 Beethoven was considering a move to Paris and felt that by entitling his third symphony "Bonaparte" he could ease his way into Parisian musical society.

   3. We know that Beethoven revoked the dedication and chose to remain in Vienna.

   4. We suspect that the image of Napoleon was used by Beethoven as part of his inspiration in writing a symphony about a heroic/mythic character battling adversity and emerging triumphant.

5. More important than Napoleon was the image of the mythic hero, Prometheus, a symbol of resistance against arbitrary authority and, by extension, of the plight of the unappreciated artist.
   a. Beethoven's ballet "The Creatures of Prometheus" was composed in 1801.
   b. The dramatic and symbolic elements of Beethoven's "Prometheus" ballet—struggle, death, rebirth and apotheosis—become the essential dramatic elements of the third symphony.
6. Most important was Beethoven's personal identification with the image of the hero struggling against adversity.

II. Symphony No. 3 in E Flat Major, Op. 55, movement 1, sonata-allegro form: analysis with reference to the WordScore Guide™ and musical examples.

A. Introduction.

Two riveting E flat major chords establish the tonic key and a royal, macho mood.

B. Theme 1 is a theme of great complexity and expressive breadth that represents the heroic image. The subsequent themes in this movement all grow out of one or another of the aspects of theme 1, which is composed of two basic elements: phrases a and b.
   1. Phrase a consists of two contrasting elements:
      a. A triadic opening. (A triad is the fundamental three-note harmony that establishes a key.)
      b. A descending step motive. (A motive is a short group of notes that may, or may not, be part of a larger theme.) The descent adds a dissonance, suggestive of darker emotions.
   2. Phrase a^1 develops the triadic element of phrase a. Beethoven has already begun to develop his theme in the exposition using the technique of sequence. A sequence is the repetition of a motive at different pitch levels.
   3. Phrase b is a development of the triadic element of phrase a, now rhythmically altered by a hemiola. A hemiola is a pattern of new accents that momentarily seems to change the existing meter, frequently from triple to duple meter. It creates rhythmic ambiguity

thereby serving to heighten tension and increase momentum. Hemiolas were a real challenge to 18th-century musicians, who were used to the much simpler rhythms of Classical Era style. They play a major role in Beethoven's heroic compositional style.

    4. Phrase a² is triumphant and magnificent.

    5. All the themes of movement 1 and its development grow out of three aspects of theme 1:

        a. The triadic element.

        b. The descending steps.

        c. The hemiola.

C. Theme 2 is in two parts.

    1. Part 1 is gentle and lyrical and based on the descending step motive of theme 1, which it develops through a series of ever-widening intervals. It appears directly out of the end of theme 1 without any intervening bridge passage.

    2. Part 2 is a gentle, rising melody, itself an inversion of the descending step motive of theme 1.

D. Theme 3 is a tender, harmonically conceived theme grown from the triadic opening of theme 1. Beethoven is breaking the classical mold with his introduction of more than two main themes. This movement alone is as long as some Classical Era symphonies in their entirety.

E. The cadence theme (theme 4) is triumphant and heroic. It too has grown from the triadic opening of theme 1. It is in five parts.

    1. Part 1 is a martial-like triadic theme marked by syncopations. (Syncopation is the disruption of the existing rhythm by accents that appear where they are not expected.)

    2. Part 2 is a rising sequence in the strings, marked by a hemiola.

    3. Part 3 is an attempt to "right" the rhythm with a three-note step descent. It does not work, and the music breaks down into a series of two-chord descending units that fragment further into a single chord.

    4. Part 4 is a rising triadic motive from theme 1.

    5. Part 5 is a brief, mysterious version of the theme 1 opening.

6. This cadence is not typical of its kind. It is almost developmental. Far from providing a satisfying conclusion to the exposition, it brings harmonic dissonance and rhythmic disruption into play.

F. The transition passage (theme 5) that appears between theme 2 and theme 3 behaves harmonically like the modulating bridge that should have (according to Classical Era rules) but did not occur between themes 1 and 2. It is characterized by descending motives with a "hoofbeat" rhythm.

G. The entire exposition section is revolutionary in its length and its disregard for established classical rules of musical form, harmony, and rhythm. Nothing like it had been done before and very little like it has been done since.

H. The development section is in 12 parts.

    1. This is the romantic core of the movement. The development can be seen as a struggle against the self, a spiritual struggle contained within the soul of the hero.

    2. The gut-wrenching climax of this struggle comes in part 7 of the development section. This is brutal music, full of dissonance and modal and rhythmic ambiguity. By stretching a nine-measure progression to 36 measures that repeat the most dissonant harmonies available to him without resolving them, and by using hemiolas, Beethoven manages to obliterate our sense of tonic, beat, and meter. A contemporary audience, accustomed to dissonance on a daily basis, may not appreciate its brutality, but the symphony's 18th-century audience would have found it shocking and deeply disturbing.

    3. Parts 1–6 constitute a long and varied buildup to the trauma that is part 7.

        a. Part 1 extends the brief, mysterious version of theme 1 heard at the end of the exposition.

        b. Part 2 brings back theme 2.

        c. Part 3 introduces a minor-mode sequence of the theme 1 opening accompanied by shivering strings.

        d. Part 4 juxtaposes the theme 1 sequence rising in the bass with the "hoofbeat" motives galloping above it.

        e. Part 5 quietly brings back theme 2, part 1.

      f.   Part 6 is the beginning of a dramatic fugue, based on the "hoofbeat" rhythm of part 4. It is brutally cut off by part 7, the development part from hell described above.

   4.   Part 8 (theme 6) is a new-sounding theme of pain and remembrance. In actuality it is a counterpoint to the triadic element of theme 1. (It is harmonically related to the triadic element of theme 1.)

   5.   Parts 9–12 leave the struggle behind as the recapitulation approaches. A distant horn presages the opening of theme 1.

I.   Recapitulation.

   1.   The dissonant C sharp of the descending step motive of theme 1 now resolves to a C natural, instantly relieving the theme of the dark tint it exhibited in the exposition.

   2.   Theme 1 proceeds without the rhythmically ambiguous phrase b.

   3.   The remainder of the recapitulation proceeds according to the regular classical format with the reappearance of themes 2 and 3 and the cadence material parts 1–5.

J.   The coda is in eight parts. It is a development of the development section. Darkness is banished and triumph reigns supreme.

   1.   In part 1 the triadic opening of theme 1 is heard three times in three subsequent keys, the keys outlining the descending step motive E flat–D flat–C. To Beethoven's contemporary audience this is an outlandishly crude harmonic sequence. Its purpose is to tie together the dissonant C sharp (D flat) of theme 1 in the exposition with the C natural of theme 1 in the recapitulation.

   2.   In part 2 the theme 1 sequence is accompanied by a melody derived from the fugue subject (part 6 of the development).

   3.   In part 3 the "new theme" from the development reappears for a necessary thematic recapitulation.

   4.   Part 4 focuses on the melody derived from the fugue subject.

   5.   Parts 5–7 focus on returns of themes 1 and 2.

6. In Part 8 a series of syncopated chords create one last hemiola. Three detached E flat major tonic chords end the movement as it began.

K. Conclusion: this movement is a metaphor for Beethoven's progression to self-awareness and control of his own destiny.

III. Beethoven's compositional innovations are:

A. Music must be a vehicle for self-expression. It is not a decorative art. It is not just for the cognoscenti or even the middle class.

B. Classical forms can and should be adapted to fit the particular context of the composition.

C. Motivic development is a basic compositional technique.

D. Rhythm and rhythmic manipulation is raised to a level of thematic and developmental importance.

E. Movements form a dramatic progression, as acts in a play.

IV. Movement 2 (Marche funèbre).

A. For whom does this funeral march toll?

1. For Napoleon? This is unlikely because Beethoven wrote movement 2 before he fell out with Napoleon.

2. Because of the rumored death of Lord Nelson? This idea, propounded 49 years after the piece was written, is also unlikely.

3. For the war dead? Again an unlikely idea since the Napoleonic wars had not really begun in earnest at this point.

4. Does the overall dramatic progression of the movements of the "Eroica" describe:

a. Beethoven's own life and struggles?

b. A universal depiction of life, struggle, and apotheosis?

5. Specifics aside, the *Marche funèbre* addresses itself generally to the subjects of heroism, sacrifice, and mourning.

B. Funeral march theme.

1. The movement begins without an introduction.

2. The theme consists of two phrases. Phrase a is a dismal and deeply pained theme in C minor. Phrase b is a broad, lyrical and brighter melody in E flat major.

3. The drum roll typical of a funeral march is supplied by the contrabasses. Beethoven did not have the requisite snare drum available. Moreover, he needed a specific pitch, something the snare drum would not have provided.

4. The theme, and the movement in general, owes a debt to French Republican band models.

Musical example: François Gossec's *Marche lugubre.*

C. Analysis of the movement in five large parts.

1. Part 1 introduces the two-phrase funeral theme, played twice.

2. Part 2 introduces the contrasting "Redemption" theme.

3. Part 3:

    a. The dismal funeral theme returns.

    b. A dramatic fugue develops. Its subject is based on the funeral theme's Phrase b. This use of a baroque form gives the movement an unexpected twist.

    c. The fugue's polyphony solidifies into a series of dissonant chords and the funeral theme returns for highly dramatic treatment evoking a terrifying vision of the final judgment.

4. Part 4 is a recapitulation of the funeral theme. It ends with a deceptive cadence that unexpectedly redirects the music to A flat major!

5. Part 5 is a five-part coda that brings back the "Redemption" theme, before a final anguished, fragmented version of the funeral march.

V. Movement 3, scherzo.

A. The scherzo offers a stunning contrast with the preceding funeral march.

B. Scherzo 1: *allegro vivace.*

1. Chattering introductory music precedes the main theme.

2. The scherzo theme (phrase a) itself is a charming, quirky tune heard initially in the oboe. It seems to be searching for a home (tonic) key.

3. A celebratory arrival of the theme in E flat major is followed by an exuberant, syncopated E flat major arpeggio (phrase b) derived from theme 1, movement 1.

4. Scherzo 1 is repeated.

C. Trio.

    1. This is initially scored for three horns and accompanimental strings (phrase c).

    2. Phrase d introduces a simple, almost rustic "long-short" rhythm.

    3. This rustic phrase is repeated.

D. Scherzo 2.

    1. This is similar to scherzo 1, until

    2. The E flat major arpeggio returns and then appears in a surprising and exhilarating duple meter. Again, we see how Beethoven uses rhythm to create a great narrative development.

    3. The coda is a brief and explosive conclusion.

VI. Movement 4, quasi-variations.

A. The fourth movement has been controversial since the premiere of the symphony. Its comic, often slapstick character has, for many, made it an inappropriate conclusion for this otherwise heroic symphony.

B. Introduction.

    1. Blaring, dramatic opening appears to signal an event of great importance.

    2. Instead, a silly, mousy little tune emerges.

    3. This theme (in the strings) indulges in a strange and comic dialogue with the rest of the orchestra.

    4. The theme appears twice more. Despite its cuteness, this theme does not sound substantial enough to carry the movement, which, as of yet, has not "gotten off the ground."

C. Master theme (the truth is revealed).

    1. The theme of the introduction reveals itself to be the bass line for an infinitely more interesting theme that now makes its appearance.

    2. Beethoven's game plan for the remainder of the movement:

        a. The master theme returns periodically, each time varied.

b. The bass theme (introduction theme) continues to assert itself on the movement, only to be humorously brushed aside by the various returns of the master theme.

c. The bass theme initiates what at first appears to be a substantial fugue.

d. This fugue is obliterated by the master theme.

e. The bass theme returns in the low strings for a march section.

f. Again the master theme returns to deflate the intentions of the bass theme.

g. Ultimately reconciled, the master theme and the bass theme appear together in a double fugue (a fugue with two subjects and one of the most complex of all baroque forms).

h. The master theme returns in a third and fourth variation.

i. The movement ends with a six-part coda that brings back the grand, fanfarish introduction to the movement in part 4. Now it leads to a thrilling conclusion in which the E flat major chords from movement 1 appear in extended form.

VII. Conclusion.

Symphony No. 3 marks Beethoven's coming of age. Upon it he built the whole of his subsequent output.

A conversation between Christian Kuffner, a poet, and Beethoven:
Kuffner: "Tell me, frankly, which is your favourite among your symphonies?"

Beethoven: "Eh! Eh! the 'Eroica.'"

(Summer, 1817)

Lecture Nine—Transcript
Symphony No. 3—The New Path—Heroism and Self-Expression, I

Welcome back to the symphonies of Beethoven. These are Lectures Nine through Twelve, and they will all deal with the incredible Symphony No. 3, and these four lectures as a group are entitled, "The New Path: Heroism and Self-Expression." Beethoven composed the bulk of his Symphony No. 3 in the year 1803. The Third Symphony is simply the key work in Beethoven's musical revolution, a revolution brought about by the events, the crisis of 1802, a crisis itself precipitated by Beethoven's seemingly incurable loss of hearing.

In the Heiligenstadt Testament of October 1802, Beethoven had written, "With joy, I hasten to meet death. If it comes before I've had a chance to develop my artistic capacities, it will still be coming too soon. Yet even so, I would be happy, for it would free me from a state of endless suffering." Indeed, in 1802 and in 1803, Beethoven was in great emotional pain. The testament is filled with apology, pride, self-pity, self-justification, and, indeed, genuine pathos. It is Beethoven's great Weltschmerz. However, as Joseph Kerman ably points out, and I quote Kerman, "The neurotic details of the Heiligenstadt Testament are not much to the point. After all, other artists have suffered neurosis, breakdown, chronic depression, extreme illness, and destructive love affairs without experiencing the amazing artistic aftereffects that such things seem to have produced in Beethoven, like the Third Symphony, for example."

What Kerman is talking about, before I continue with this quote, should be obvious to all of us folks. Beethoven is deeply depressed, very unhappy, almost suicidal at moments in 1802, yet this seems to inspire him. This seems to work him up into an entirely new phase of creative power and imagination. Many of us fold under this sort of emotional pressure; with Beethoven, this sort of dark emotional negativity seemed to act as a catalyst. What a strange and marvelous way to deal with very dark emotions and feelings, and it was just Beethoven and our good luck that he would respond in such a way.

Back to Joseph Kerman; "The Third Symphony is a watershed work, not only in terms of Beethoven's own music but, indeed, also in terms of our whole musical tradition considered as broadly as we please. With his simple but unerring sense of symbolism, Beethoven had inscribed the piece to Napoleon, as it is very well known, and then tore up the title page when he saw Napoleon betray the revolution. But Beethoven did not to tear up the symphony. And after the Third, there was no more chance of going back to the classical style than there was to the *ancien regime* itself. After the "Eroica," Beethoven's music breathes in a different world than that of the 1790s."

Let's talk about what the "Eroica" is, and perhaps is not, about. We know that Beethoven's feelings about Napoleon were ambivalent, as they were regarding anyone he perceived as an authority figure. We know that Beethoven was considering in 1803 a move to Paris; by naming his new Third Symphony "Bonaparte," he felt he could ease his way into Parisian musical society. We know that Beethoven revoked the dedication to Napoleon after he decided to remain in Vienna. We've suspected that Napoleon—or the heroic image of Napoleon—was used by Beethoven as a catalyst in writing a piece about a heroic mythic character, a character battling adversity and emerging at the end triumphant, although clearly this heroic character is more Mr. Beethoven himself than it is Napoleon.

Even more important than Napoleon to the genesis of the Third Symphony was the image of the mythic hero Prometheus. Beethoven's ballet, "The Creatures of Prometheus," Op. 43, was completed in 1801 in collaboration with a dance master named Salvatore Vigano. Musicologist and Beethoven scholar William Kinderman tells us this:

"The Prometheus music was Beethoven's first major work for the stage and one of his earliest public successes. The version of the Prometheus myth Beethoven and Vigano tackled reinterprets the ancient tale of the defiant champion of humanity in a manner compatible with the tenets of the Enlightenment. Prometheus ennobled humankind through his gifts of knowledge and art, fashioned from the fire that he had stolen from the gods. In all versions of the myth, Prometheus in severely punished for his actions on behalf of humanity. In the original version, Prometheus is chained to a rock where an eagle descends to devour his liver. (Yes indeed, ouch!)

"However, though physically chained, Prometheus is spiritually free. In the world of myth, there is no more telling symbol of resistance to the arbitrary exercise of authority than Prometheus. In the version

Beethoven set to music, Prometheus' trials in agony are replaced by a progression of death and rebirth. This version of the myth shifts the dramatic emphasis from the defiant marker to the reception by humankind of the Promethean gift of culture. In the ballet that Beethoven provided the music for, the cultural gifts are not immediately understood or appreciated. Consequently, Prometheus' agony comes to parallel the plight of the misunderstood artist." I would point out that theme of the fourth movement of the Third Symphony is borrowed from the Prometheus ballet.

William Kinderman concludes: "The dramatic and symbolic elements borrowed from the Prometheus myth are by no means confined to the finale of the Third Symphony. The overall narrative progression of the four movements of the symphony outline a sequence of events, and that sequence of events is this. In the first movement, we could say struggle is the essential topic. In the second movement of the Third Symphony, death is the essential topic. In the third movement, rebirth; in the fourth movement, apotheosis. The parallel of the Third Symphony with Beethoven's own despair, his own thoughts of suicide, and his own discovery of a new artistic path is scarcely accidental. But the mythic heroic symbolism of Prometheus must be considered as important an influence on Beethoven's Third Symphony as his own biography and as the influence of Napoleon.

What Beethoven explores in the Third Symphony are universal aspects of heroism, centering on the idea of confrontation with adversity, leading ultimately to a renewal of creative possibilities. What really counts, after all, of this lovely but highfalutin' analysis is: Does Beethoven say this in the music, and, if he does, how does he say it in the music? He does, and he says it brilliantly, so let's dive into this massive first movement and examine this marvelous hero he creates out of the first theme, the struggles that hero undergoes in the development section, and ultimately the victory won in the coda of this first movement. It's very literary music, yet it still is brilliantly composed so that it makes sense simply as music unto itself. We can interpret it many different ways, and I'll do my best to give us a rounded view of this movement.

Onward and offward, please. We start at the very beginning with the briefest of brief introductions. This movement is in sonata-allegro form—again, every one of Beethoven's first movements of every one of his nine symphonies is in sonata-allegro form. This is Op. 55 in E flat major. Let's listen to what passes for an introduction to this movement.

Musical example from Symphony No. 3 in E Flat Major, Op. 55, movement 1

That's it. Let me read from your WordScore. Introduction, and in the WordScores I put quotations around the word "introduction" because this happened so quickly: "It's hard to even notice it as something special, but it is. More like a harmonic preface, two riveting tonic E flat major chords establish both the tonic E flat and the powerfully royal and frankly macho mood. Royal and harmonically absolute, Beethoven tells us this is the beginning and this is my key."

Musical example from Symphony No. 3 in E Flat Major, Op. 55, movement 1

It's unequivocal and very powerful, with the entire orchestra helping to pronounce these harmonies. When we compare this introduction to the long narrative affairs of the first and second symphonies, we realize it's a very different kettle of fish entirely. I would also point out, as I did when we studied the First Symphony, that that symphony begins with an ambiguity, with a dissonance in its first harmony—no dissonance here; an absolute statement of E flat major. Here I am; this is what I am. Listen to it again

Musical example from Symphony No. 3 in E Flat Major, Op. 55, movement 1

We're going to need that clean pronouncement of E flat major because in just moments, Beethoven's going to get into all kinds of marvelous ambiguous trouble, so having clearly established where we're starting from, let us now start to examine, very slowly, this huge and fascinating first theme.

Theme 1, and I read from your WordScores: "A theme of stunning motific, harmonic, and rhythmic complexity and expressive breadth, theme 1 personifies the hero, and its motives will sire (that is, its motives will give birth) to the other themes in the movement. As a result, the other themes are not so much contrasts with theme 1 as they are different facets of the same rich, heroic personality." Theme 1 has four basic phrases; I've given them the rather unromantic names of phrase A, A prime, B, and A double prime. That's all right.

We can call them what we want; it's the music that counts. Let us first listen to the theme from the intro through its four phrases in its entirety, just to get it in our ear, and then we will go back and talk about each phrase individually and listen cumulatively until we really have come to know this first theme quite intimately, but, first, introduction and theme 1. I will indicate the phrases as they occur.

Musical example from Symphony No. 3 in E Flat Major, Op. 55, movement 1

Phrase A.

Musical example from Symphony No. 3 in E Flat Major, Op. 55, movement 1

A prime.

Musical example from Symphony No. 3 in E Flat Major, Op. 55, movement 1

Phrase B.

Musical example from Symphony No. 3 in E Flat Major, Op. 55, movement 1

A double prime.

Musical example from Symphony No. 3 in E Flat Major, Op. 55, movement 1

Let's get to know this theme with great intimacy so that it becomes printed behind our eyelids. Phrase A, and I refer to your WordScores: "A lyric of magic majesty emerges, consisting of two essential motific ideas." I would remind you what a motive is—it's a very important word. A motive is a brief succession of pitches out of which melody or theme can grow through the processes of sequence repetition or transformation.

Beethoven is a motive composer; he loves short, compact motific ideas that can be spawned and woven into always new-sounding themes but can always be traced backwards to their original source. By composing with motives, Beethoven is able to weave these very ornate tapestries that are always united but always grow from one or two early and familiar sources. Back to my description: "A theme of lyric majesty emerges consisting of two essential motific ideas: a broad triadic opening, followed by an incredible and dissonant chromatic step descent from E flat to C sharp."

Let me explain. In previous lectures, we've talked about Beethoven's propensity for writing opening themes that are triadic, that outline the basic comic chord or some other chord. Triadic theme simply means that Beethoven is taking the harmony, a triad…

[Chord on piano]

…and outlining that harmony melodically.

[Notes on piano]

Or, in this case…

[Notes on piano]

…this allows Beethoven to start as unambiguously in melody as he did harmonically.

[Notes on piano]

To the opening melodic phrase, this broad and frankly heroic opening phrase, played, by the way, by the orchestral cellos which imbue it with a further sense of masculinity, this opening melodic phrase reflects the opening harmonic attacks in the introduction and clearly expresses a sense of peace and repose via E flat major. That's the first important motive.

[Notes on piano]

And wherever you are, I want you to sing that. That's motive 1. But immediately following on the tails of motive 1, this good-feeling, broad, masculine idea is a very tightly wound and frankly dissonant melodic idea.

[Notes on piano]

We call it chromatic because it outlines on a piano a black note to a white note to a black note, all adjacent to each other. It's a very tight melodic idea, and it leads to a very different and dissonant harmonic place.

[Notes on piano]

A whole G minor world of darkness is implied by that downward…

[Notes on piano]

…descending step motive. It is not a happy sound, and it imbues this opening phrase with great ambiguity, because what's this music about? Is it open and broad and heroic, or is tightly wound, chromatic, ambiguous and dark? Or is it both? Indeed, it is both. We have the seeds, just hearing phrase A, of broad and rogue masculinity and dark and despairing unhappiness, as represented by the dissonance of that descending step motive. It's a marvelous bit of slight of hand by Beethoven, both light and dark, heroic and despairing, present virtually at the same time, virtually in the same theme. Dissonance and consonance co-exist within the soul of this most heroic theme.

Let's listen again to the introduction and theme 1, but this time just phrase A of theme 1, and please notice as best as you can that broad opening triadic motive and then the dissonance and darkness implicit in the [singing] that follows, because these are ideas that will play out across the broad span of the movement. Introduction.

Musical example from Symphony No. 3 in E Flat Major, Op. 55, movement 1

As phrase A concludes, we spin back to E flat major, and we might think that this brief foray into darkness and minor and that strange C sharp we heard, we might forget it ever happened. What was that? A bit of undigested potato perhaps, but nothing that we can worry about or should worry about. The darkness implicit in that first phrase will come back in time later in the movement, so let's remember it was there, despite the fact we're back in E flat major at the advent of phrase A prime.

I read from your WordScores: "A prime: once the key of E flat major has been re-attained, Beethoven immediately begins extending developing various aspects of the theme. This phrase A prime sees the triadic element of the theme of phrase A isolated and sequence upwards." I would remind you that a sequence is when we take a motive and repeat it, but at higher or lower pitch levels. Therefore, this is a sequence.

[Notes on piano]

The second idea having been on lower pitches than the first, this is not a sequence.

[Notes on piano]

That was simple repetition of the same idea on the same pitches. Sequence is an essential way of making an idea move forward, yet obtaining the integrity of that idea. As we repeat an idea at different pitch levels, we need new harmonies to underpin it, and there's a sense of movement and progression, but melodically we still recognize where we are. So sequence is an essential technique for extending melodic ideas.

In any case, what Beethoven does in phrase A prime is extend that opening triadic motive via sequence. He starts developing his theme right away, right here in theme 1, not in the development section, not in the coda, but immediately after having stated it. This is what phrase A prime sounds like.

[Notes on piano]

Let me do that for you again, and again, notice it's the same idea, but ever higher ratcheting upwards into the musical stratosphere.

[Notes on piano]

Beethoven is developing the theme virtually as he goes. Please, let us listen now to the introduction, phrase A and phrase A prime. I want you to notice the marvelous and macho opening chords. I want you to perceive both the broad and bright opening, and then the dark descent into C sharp, and then I want you to be aware of the development of that opening broad triadic motive in phrase A prime. Introduction.

Musical example from Symphony No. 3 in E Flat Major, Op. 55, movement 1

A prime.

Musical example from Symphony No. 3 in E Flat Major, Op. 55, movement 1

Phrase B. The triadic element of the theme isolated and extended in phrase A prime is now further developed. It is inverted and elongated. And let me explain what I mean by inverted first. In phrase A prime, we heard that sequential progression of motive 1 as it went upwards in the orchestra.

Musical example from Symphony No. 3 in E Flat Major, Op. 55, movement 1

Phrase B begins by simply taking the triadic and sending it downwards.

Musical example from Symphony No. 3 in E Flat Major, Op. 55, movement 1

Same idea, but now what went up goes down. What makes phrase B really interesting is not the melodic manipulation but the rhythmic manipulation. To this falling motive, a new element is added: rhythmic disruption via hemiola. Hemiola, it's a nasty sounding word, vaguely reminds me of a dermatological problem, which we won't get into right now. For those of you watching, you can see the spelling on the board. For those of you listening, I would tell you it is h-e-m-i-o-l-a. It is one of those words that will help crossword puzzle doers forever; you will never find it in a crossword dictionary. In any case, what a hemiola is, and I will define it now, what it really is is a pattern of syncopation that creates the illusion that we've changed meter. I've just used a bunch of terms, and I'll explain them all.

First, syncopation: Syncopation is when we have an accent on a beat we don't expect to be accented. This movement, this first movement of Beethoven's Third Symphony, is in what we call triple meter. That means we're hearing an accent, a powerful accent, every third beat. Like a waltz, we're hearing ONE-two-three, ONE-two-three. We hear three beats, and the next is accented, then two unaccented and then another accented. It makes us hear beats grouped in three. ONE-two-three, ONE-two-three and so forth, so a syncopation is when we have an accent somewhere we don't expect it.

For example, what if Beethoven started accenting the second beats or the third beats? Before long, this might not sound like triple meter anymore, and, indeed, that's what happens in hemiola. A hemiola is a pattern of syncopations, a pattern of accents that creates the illusion that you've changed meter. For example, what would happen if, instead of accenting one in triple meter, Beethoven accents instead, for a brief period of time, the third beat and then the second beat of the next measure, the first, third and second beats, rather than just the first? This is what we get: ONE-two-three, ONE-two-three, one-two-THREE, one-TWO-three, one-two-THREE, one-TWO-three. Sounds like twos. That's what a hemiola is, a pattern of accent that momentarily seems to change the meter, usually from three to two.

If one continues doing this for too long, the ear will say, "Meter has changed," but if you keep going back and forth, it creates great rhythmic stress, great rhythmic ambiguity. Our insides start to broil because our bodies get used to a meter. Whether we're sitting or standing or doing whatever we're doing, when we hear a powerful rhythm, and we hear very powerful rhythms in Beethoven, when we hear a strongly felt meter, our bodies acclimate themselves to that meter. We dance at that meter. Whether you're moving or not, you could still be dancing. Your kidneys could be doing all kinds of moves all over their internal dance floor. When we mess with time, when we mess with meter, it creates great stress and great ambiguity, and that's what Beethoven does in phrase B.

We enter phrase B, clearly in triple meter, and then he starts introducing all kinds of hemiolas, all kinds of accentuation that would seem to be changing the meter. I'll just sing you the rhythm of phrase B, then we'll listen to it, and listen to it again, but just the rhythm and phrase B. [singing] Accents all over the place, accentuation everywhere, meter changes! I would tell you that on an opening night performance, an orchestra unaccustomed to this almost Stravinskian sense of unanticipated accents would go bonkers. This would be very hard music in 1803, fairly easy today, but in 1803, very hard.

Another thing I would tell you is that one reason why Beethoven is still such a contemporary-sounding composer for us today is that his rhythmic surfaces, this kind of manipulation is very contemporary. We're used to this in rock and roll. We're used to this in jazz. We're used to this rhythmic dislocation and disruption in our lives all the time in the late 20th century. But we don't hear much of this in the music of the Classical or even the early Romantic Era. Time is felt to be a steadier and more regular thing in this age, but for Beethoven, time is not a steady and regular thing. He was a very 20th-century person in this way. His internal disruption gets well translated into this kind of rhythmic manipulation, and we're going to hear it here on out until the end of this course.

Let us listen to phrase B, which begins as a descending development of the opening motive from phrase A but quickly becomes dominated by this rhythmic manipulation. Phrase B.

Musical example from Symphony No. 3 in E Flat Major, Op. 55, movement 1

What we will do is listen to the introductory chords, phrase A, phrase A prime, and phrase B. Slowly we're putting all this back together, and when we get to phrase B—you will forgive me—I will count along with these strange accents and indicate where we are in phrase B, and then we will finish this theme and move forward. The introduction

Musical example from Symphony No. 3 in E Flat Major, Op. 55, movement 1

Phrase A.

Musical example from Symphony No. 3 in E Flat Major, Op. 55, movement 1

A prime.

Musical example from Symphony No. 3 in E Flat Major, Op. 55, movement 1

Which brings us finally to phrase A double prime. I read from your WordScores: "Triumphant and magnificent, the heroic theme celebrates via the triadic element the re-attainment of the downbeat. If phrase A prime celebrated the re-attainment of E flat major, now we can finally celebrate knowing where the beat is again, and our bodies can again rest secure that they know where the downbeat should be and where it belongs—and with it, by the way, rhythmic stability." Note there is no step descent, no C sharp lying dissonance here to cloud this marvelous and victorious music. This phrase A double prime celebrates the E flat major and rhythmic stability, two things which are going to be brought into great question as we move through this movement. It is the hero in control of himself, at least for now.

Let us listen then to the entire theme in its entirety, those magnificent and powerful and unambiguous opening chords which express clearly both mood and E flat major, phrase A, with its broad opening motive, but also that descending chromatic, that descent that creates great dissonance and ambiguity, light side and dark side, phrase A prime, immediately developing the broad opening triad, phrase B, developing further the broad opening triad, but more than that, introducing the element of rhythmic ambiguity. Phrase A double prime brings it all together. The opening motives are intact; we're back in E flat major. We celebrate momentarily a theme in control.

Musical example from Symphony No. 3 in E Flat Major, Op. 55, movement 1

Phrase A.

Musical example from Symphony No. 3 in E Flat Major, Op. 55, movement 1

A prime.

Musical example from Symphony No. 3 in E Flat Major, Op. 55, movement 1

B.

Musical example from Symphony No. 3 in E Flat Major, Op. 55, movement 1

A double prime.

Musical example from Symphony No. 3 in E Flat Major, Op. 55, movement 1

We should have a sense at A double prime we made it, we made it out of that rhythmic hole. We'll be in others very soon, but there's a sense of victory, a sense of accomplishment having made it through that theme.

This is a very complex and long theme. It represents the hero; it is indeed Beethoven's hero. The hero has a rich and complex personality. He (or it, you make your choice) is in turns explosive and macho, richly masculine with both a light and dark side, developmental, rhythmically ambiguous and ultimately our hero. Our theme is triumphant.

The other themes in this movement, and this is the key to understanding this first movement, the other themes in this movement, and there are as many as six of them, depending on how you count them, as well as the developmental material, all grow out of one or another of the motific aspects of theme 1. I'm going to say this again because it's so important. All the themes of this movement and the developmental material all grow out of one or another of the motific aspects of theme 1. They either grow out of the triadic portion of theme 1, the descending step motive of theme 1, or the hemiola that we heard in phrase B of theme 1.

We should think, therefore, of all the themes that follow theme 1 in this movement as facets of, as extensions of, as developments of theme 1, all as being part of the same complex personality that it is, Beethoven's magnificent and troubled hero. Whatever contrast we hear, we should hear it as contrast within a single personality. Whatever differences we should hear within the themes, we should understand as differences within a single personality. The hero, theme 1, spawns all of the other themes; all of the other themes are aspects of the hero. For example, theme 2, a lyric theme in two parts, we hear it without any modulatory music between theme 1 and theme 2. We simply go from E flat major to the B flat major of theme 2. Let's listen to it first in its entirety. It is in two parts. I will indicate the parts as we hear them. Theme 2.

Musical example from Symphony No. 2 in E Flat Major, movement 1

Part 2.

Musical example from Symphony No. 2 in E Flat Major, movement 1

Let's talk about the derivation of theme 2, because I've already told you it's going to grow out of some aspect of theme 1. Theme 2 is spawned from the step descent of theme 1. Part 1, gentle lyric theme, appears directly out of the end of theme 1 without any intervening bridge passage. The theme consists of a series of light-as-a-feather, three-note descents derived from the step descent of theme 1, and this first part of the second theme ends with a vigorous orchestral descent, based itself on this step descent.

We'll get to that in a moment but, first, let's just talk again about the derivation of this theme. We look to Beethoven's sketchbooks, to the earliest appearance of what probably is (in fact, what is) the second theme to help us understand the derivation. The first appearance of this first part of theme 2 sounds like this, as it appears in an early sketchbook.

[Notes on piano]

It's one of these typical Beethovenian sketches, this absolutely banal "three blind mice." How Beethoven's going to build a marvelous and memorable theme out of this, we have to watch the intervening steps. But this is the first appearance of theme 2 in any sketchbook. The next appearance is a slightly more interesting and more complex version.

[Notes on piano]

26   ©1998 The Teaching Company.

That's the next version of theme 2 that appears in a sketchbook, and indeed that's much closer to what we end up with, and what we end up with, the final version, is as follows.

[Notes on piano]

The derivation of this theme should be clear to us; the descending step motive from theme 1 went like this.

[Notes on piano]

Let's just play that up higher.

[Notes on piano]

And let's re-rhythmicize it.

[Notes on piano]

There's our opening of theme 2, and what theme 2 now does is takes that descending step motive, begins with it, and progressively widens it, makes it broader and broader, developing this step motive to a series of progressive expansions. I explain. The first version of the step motive is as it appeared in theme 1.

[Notes on piano]

It spans a distance of what we call a minor third. But the next appearance spans the distance of what we call a perfect fourth. It's a little wider.

[Notes on piano]

Then, an augmented fourth.

[Notes on piano]

Then, a seventh, seven notes

[Notes on piano]

Each time those three notes are heard, they're outlining a wider chunk of musical space. Then he goes back to the minor third again.

[Notes on piano]

Now he outlines five notes.

[Notes on piano]

He outlines six notes.

[Notes on piano]

And so forth.

[Notes on piano]

Finishing by outlining six notes. For every time we hear this three-note motive in theme 2, it starts as we heard it in the first theme, but each time we hear it in theme 2, it gets wider and wider and wider, broader and broader. He's developing as he goes. This is very exciting, because he's taking an idea that we heard at the very beginning of the piece, re-using in a way that it sounds unfamiliar, and then developing it into what sounds like a brand new theme, but is retracing back. It's not new at all. It grows out of theme 1.

Let us listen to theme 2, just part 1, and let's be aware of this progressive expansion by which he takes an earlier motive, adapts it into a new format and creates a new sounding theme. Theme 2, part 1.

Musical example from Symphony No. 3 in E Flat Major, Op. 55, movement 1

Theme 2, part 2 inverts the vigorous orchestral descent of a major sixth, which concluded part 1, which itself is an outgrowth of the descending step motive, and I would remind you that that vigorous descent sounded like this.

[Notes on piano]

It simply inverts that. Instead of going down, it goes up.

[Notes on piano]

That's just a straight inversion, but that's all Beethoven need do to create a new-sounding theme, itself an outgrowth of theme 1 step motive, to create a gentle, rising melody. The music quickly becomes more dramatic and animated. Please listen to theme 2, part 2. Let's be aware that this rising music simply is an inversion of the falling music we just heard at the end of part 1 of theme 2, which itself grew out of an opening motive heard in theme 1. But theme 2, part 2.

Musical example from Symphony No. 3 in E Flat Major, Op. 55, movement 1

And now let us listen to theme 2 in its entirety, starting with the descending step motive, ever expanding it, until we reach a point in part 1 of theme 2 where we have that long descent of a sixth, then inverting that sixth into theme 2, part 2. Theme 2.

Musical example from Symphony No. 3 in E Flat Major, Op. 55, movement 1

Part 2.

Musical example from Symphony No. 3 in E Flat Major, Op. 55, movement 1

This is the game we're going to play as we move through this movement and examining the themes. We're going to examine their derivations, and their derivations start with theme 1 always.

Theme 3, you might be thinking, "I thought sonata movements only had two main themes." Yes, usually, but this is what my daughter might call a heck'a sonata-form movement. That's what an earlier generation might have called a mega sonata-form movement, or just a darn big one. Beethoven's got a lot of themes, a lot on his developmental plate, a big coda. This is a very long movement, nearly 700 measures in length. This single movement is as long as some Classical Era symphonies. Onward to theme 3. I read from your WordScores: Theme 3 is spawned from the triadic harmonic element of theme 1. It is a tender, harmonically conceived theme, made up of repeated triadically ascending harmonies. Which aspect of theme 1 is theme 3 built on? This part.

[Notes on piano]

The triadic aspect. Theme 3 sounds like this.

[Notes on piano]

It just outlines the harmony; that's all it does. And, of course, he harmonizes this theme with these repeated chords.

[Notes on piano]

It grows directly out of the triadic root of theme 1. I continue reading from your WordScore at measure 99: The groups of three repeated chords give way to groups of two, and at measure 103 the momentarily quiet, gentle respite is over. Staccato, which means very sharply attacked strings, initiate a rapidly developing transition. There's a crescendo, which means to get louder, and we're going to go to another musical place. But meanwhile, theme 3 in its entirety, starting with measure 84.

Musical example from Symphony No. 3 in E Flat Major, Op. 55, movement 1

Measure 99.

Musical example from Symphony No. 3 in E Flat Major, Op. 55, movement 1

103.

Musical example from Symphony No. 3 in E Flat Major, Op. 55, movement 1

And now we arrive at another theme. I'm not calling it theme 4, although we could. I'll call it the cadence theme, because it initiates the closing material that will finally bring this long exposition to its conclusion. The cadence theme is spawned from the triadic element of theme 1. I read from your WordScore: "Triumphant, heroic, triadic theme has, despite the triple meter, a distinctly martial, march-like character," and indeed it does. It goes like this.

[Notes on piano]

It's filled with syncopations, which do not so much change the meter as imbue it with a sense of energy and forward momentum. These syncopations, however, will soon, in the cadence material, bring us to a rather dark place, but for now they're very exciting.

In the moments I have left to me in this lecture, I would read through our WordScores and talk about the ensuing cadence material, and when we come back for Lecture Two [in this section] we'll start listening to this cadence material. We'll listen to it twice because it's very diverse and very remarkable. Cadence material, part 2, the cadence theme being part 1, furious strings play a rising sequence. Note the hemiola—more rhythmic disruption. This is going to get tough. The rhythm is being significantly disrupted. Part 3, the music tries to right itself with a three-note step descent, but it doesn't work. The music breaks down into a series of two chord-descending units. The two chord units break into a single chord, heard in hemiola. Part 4, rising triadic motive from theme 1 saves the day. Falling arpeggios, triads of three notes each are heard three times, measure 144, and then at 147, huge tutti, dissonance, A diminished seven chords, and they will sound like this, and, boy! they are dissonant.

[Notes on piano]

Act to reestablish the harmony B flat, which is where we are now.

[Notes on piano]

They are a grim equivalent to the opening two E flat chords, and then part 5, a brief and mysterious version of theme 1 opening. This is a lot of information, and I'm just barking it out at you. When we come back for Lecture Two [in this section], we'll move carefully through this cadence material and see, even now, some of the ramifications of the rhythmic and harmonic ambiguity that were evidenced by the first theme. But let us take a break first.

Lecture Ten—Transcript
Symphony No. 3—The New Path—Heroism and Self-Expression, II

Welcome back to the symphonies of Beethoven. We are now at Lecture Ten, which puts us one-quarter way through our four-lecture examination of the "Eroica" Symphony, the Symphony No. 3. These four lectures together are entitled "The New Path—Heroism and Self-Expression."

Where we left off, we had just read through our WordScores apropos of the extraordinary and very complex cadence material that closes the exposition. Usually a cadence section, cadence material, has the role of bringing the exposition to a convincing and satisfactory conclusion. This cadence material goes much further than that. It is almost developmental in the way it introduces rhythmic and harmonic dissonance, drawn from theme 1, into the closing material. Even here, before the development section, the ramifications of the hemiolas of theme 1 and the harmonic dissonance of theme 1, especially the descending step motive, start coming to bear, coming to play, so what's supposed to be a satisfactory conclusion becomes a very complex and dramatic chunk of music.

We will listen to the cadence material one time through, and I'll indicate the parts; then we'll talk about it in some more detail and listen to it a second time through. It begins with that stirring and martial cadence theme, part 1, which itself is built from the triadic element of theme 1. So let's listen to the cadence material in five parts, go back, talk about it a little more, and listen to it a second time. Part 1.

Musical example from Symphony No. 3 in E Flat Major, Op. 55, movement 1

Part 2.

Musical example from Symphony No. 3 in E Flat Major, Op. 55, movement 1

Part 3.

Musical example from Symphony No. 3 in E Flat Major, Op. 55, movement 1

Measure 128.

Musical example from Symphony No. 3 in E Flat Major, Op. 55, movement 1

Part 4.

Musical example from Symphony No. 3 in E Flat Major, Op. 55, movement 1

Measure 144.

Musical example from Symphony No. 3 in E Flat Major, Op. 55, movement 1

Part 5.

Musical example from Symphony No. 3 in E Flat Major, Op. 55, movement 1

Now that we've heard it once, let's go through it again with a little more detail. Again, a stirring cadence theme, martial, drawn, indeed built on the triadic element of theme 1, leads to the beginnings of a breakdown in part 2. Furious strings play a rising sequence, but hemiola is intruding once again. Instead of hearing ONE-two-three, ONE-two three, we're hearing ONE-two, one-TWO, one-TWO, one-TWO. In part 3, the music tries to right itself by giving us a full three-note step descent. Does the music right itself? No, instead we start getting gaps. Rest-two-three, rest-two-three, and then at measure 128, a huge hemiola, these pounding, banging chords that have no context in triple meter. It's very exciting, it's very thrilling, and it creates a tremendous amount of tension, narrative tension, and ambiguity.

Finally part 4 saves the day; a rising triadic motive drawn from theme 1 brings us back to triple meter. But still we're not out of the woods yet, because we start hearing at measure 144 falling ideas which lead to that very dissonant series of harmonies that I played for you before.

[Notes on piano]

Tremendous harmonic dissonance, which only rights itself at the very end…

[Chord on piano]

…of this cadence material. It's a very complex chunk of closing music. Frankly, any other composer would have been overjoyed to call this their development section. But for Beethoven, it's simply starting to play out ramifications of theme 1, which will become extremely apparent in the development section itself. So, again, the cadence material beginning with the stirring and martial cadence theme.

Musical example from Symphony No. 3 in E Flat Major, Op. 55, movement 1

Part 2.

Musical example from Symphony No. 3 in E Flat Major, Op. 55, movement 1

Part 3.

Musical example from Symphony No. 3 in E Flat Major, Op. 55, movement 1

Measure 128.

Musical example from Symphony No. 3 in E Flat Major, Op. 55, movement 1

Part 4.

Musical example from Symphony No. 3 in E Flat Major, Op. 55, movement 1

144.

Musical example from Symphony No. 3 in E Flat Major, Op. 55, movement 1

Part 5.

Musical example from Symphony No. 3 in E Flat Major, Op. 55, movement 1

One more bit of business before we can listen to the entire exposition straight on through, and that bit of business is the transition passage that occurs at measure 65. It behaves like the modulating bridge we never had. I would point out in particular part 1 of the transition passage, because often this is referred to as theme 5, stirring, descending hoofbeat motives. The reason why they sound like cavalry or hoofbeat motives has to do with the rhythm. Yes, this is typically the hoofbeat sound we hear whenever a composer wants to evoke a sense of a charge, a cavalry and so forth, and that's the rhythm of this transition. It's the only vaguely Napoleonic or at least military thing we hear in this first movement as far as I'm concerned. They lead the transitional charge to the second part of this transition. Royally sweeping strings lead to a vigorous orchestral descent, which spans over two octaves, and that's what delivers us to the very peaceful and frankly romantic theme 3. Let's just listen to that transition passage part 1, the hoofbeat theme, theme 5.

Musical example from Symphony No. 3 in E Flat Major, Op. 55, movement 1

We've got enough in our ears to listen to the entire exposition, so now it's time to put this all together. In listening to it, let us be aware, again, of the key factor. Everything grows out of theme 1 and the three disparate elements of theme 1: the heroic and broad and light—I don't mean light in terms of lightweight, but light in terms of brilliant opening triadic motives, the dark and constricted step descent that brings us to a very different place emotionally, and the hemiolas, the rhythmic disruption associated with phrase B of theme 1. These three elements of theme 1 create every other thematic entity, indeed the cadential entity as well of this exposition. So from beginning to end, and then let us remember that in proper performance this entire exposition would be repeated, but we will not hear it repeated. We'll simply hear it one time through.

Musical example from Symphony No. 3 in E Flat Major, Op. 55, movement 1

Theme 2.

Musical example from Symphony No. 3 in E Flat Major, Op. 55, movement 1

Transition.

Musical example from Symphony No. 3 in E Flat Major, Op. 55, movement 1

Theme 3.

Musical example from Symphony No. 3 in E Flat Major, Op. 55, movement 1

Cadence theme.

Musical example from Symphony No. 3 in E Flat Major, Op. 55, movement 1

Part 2.

Musical example from Symphony No. 3 in E Flat Major, Op. 55, movement 1

Part 3.

Musical example from Symphony No. 3 in E Flat Major, Op. 55, movement 1

Part 4.

Musical example from Symphony No. 3 in E Flat Major, Op. 55, movement 1

Part 5.

Musical example from Symphony No. 3 in E Flat Major, Op. 55, movement 1

Of this extraordinary exposition, George Grove wrote in 1896 in his book, *The Beethoven Symphonies*, "There we have the chief materials of the first half of the first movement, but the way they are expressed and connected—the sunlight and cloud, the alternate fury and tenderness, the nobility, the beauty, the obstinacy, the human character—certainly nothing like it was ever done in the music before, and very little like it has been done in the 90 years since 1803," or in the 190 years since 1803.

Let's bring ourselves to the development section now. The development section is indeed the dramatic core of this movement, its, if you'll excuse me, sonar plexus. The development section represents the struggle, the confrontation with darkness and adversity, and since the development section is based on musical materials drawn entirely from theme 1, we realize that this is a struggle against the self, a physical and spiritual struggle contained within the soul of the hero, which is theme 1.

At the midpoint of the development section, part 7, we meet the gut-wrenching climax of the struggle. And if you would look at part 7 of your WordScores at measure 248, development part from hell. The preceding fugue, a dark enough bit of music in its own right, is brutally cut off by this genuinely brutal music. This incredible passage, filled with dissonance, modal ambiguity (that means we can't tell whether it's major or minor), and rhythmic ambiguity, hemiolas, represents the abyss and forms the dramatic crux of the movement. It is heard fortissimo, very loudly. Please, let's just listen to that portion of part 7, the core, the crux, the middle of the struggle.

Musical example from Symphony No. 3 in E Flat Major, Op. 55, movement 1

We are so accustomed to brutal music, we are so accustomed to dissonance of all kinds, that maybe we don't hear how ugly this music is. I'll make us hear how ugly this music is. This is brutal, ugly music of negation, because it has nothing to it except its brutal dissonance.

If this were a class on music appreciation and we were learning listening skills and I was giving an exam and said to my students, "I want you to tell me, in the next musical example, what's the meter—that is, are things happening in groups of two or three?—what's the mode? is it major or minor? what's the theme? where's the melody?" and I played this music, my students would be justified in abusing me soundly, and preferably not, but perhaps even physically abusing me, because who can tell? Is this major or minor? I don't know. Is this double or triple? I don't know. Where's the beat? I don't know. Where is this music going? Who knows? It's just music of negation.

Let me explain why. First, let's talk about its harmonic dissonance. Antony Hopkins cleverly points out that in Handel's music c. 1740, this same passage might sound something like this.

[Notes on piano]

That makes perfect sense, and that doesn't sound like music of negation, because contained within the nine measures of that Handelian example I just played we hear these dissonant harmonies, the same dissonant harmonies we heard in Beethoven, as having a functional relevance. They progress one to the next, and we perceive that progression because each harmony only takes up one measure's worth of time. But Beethoven elongates this nine-measure progression to a 36-measure passage. The first measure of this Handelian progression, and, again, I would play you that once again.

[Notes on piano]

It takes up, in Beethoven's development section, six full measures, six measures of hemiola-filled music.

[Notes on piano]

All of that was that first harmony. As a result, let's play that in real time, just that first harmony.

Musical example from Symphony No. 3 in E Flat Major, Op. 55, movement 1

What Beethoven has done, he's augmented, he's lengthened the lengths of these harmonic dissonances and then exposed them to rhythmic dissonance. He's made them into hemiolas, to the point that we don't perceive these as chords in a progression. We simply perceive them as dissonance only. They take up too much space; we don't hear the connection from one to the next, dissonance for its own sake, without the sense of impending resolution such dissonance ordinarily anticipates. What are the precedents for these amazingly sustained and repeated harmonies? How about the very beginning of the piece?

[Notes on piano]

The first thing Beethoven did was take up two measures of space with a single E flat major chord. That's a game he's played before, and the hemiolas in which we hear these incredible dissonances expressed in part 7, well, we know that hemiola has been an essential element of this piece since phrase B of theme 1. There's nothing new happening here, but he's extending the ideas to the point where all we hear is the dissonance and no sense of harmonic progression and it creates a sense of loss. We're lost; we don't know where the music's going. We don't know what the rhythm is anymore because everything is exposed to hemiola. We can't sense even beat, meter, mode, or melody. All we hear is dissonance. It's an amazing, gut-wrenching and very brave section of music for Beethoven to write because it pushes his listeners really way past anywhere they ever would have been before.

I read the complete end of part 7 from your WordScores, because after this gut-wrenching series of repeated dissonances, a series of crisp, repeated chords act like a lifeline in a stormy sea. Meter and tonality are reestablished, and we wait to see what, if anything, has survived the onslaught of part 7. Now, let's listen to part 7 again, filled with these hemiolas, which I will count for you, and then we'll hear that tag, that conclusion, this crisp series of repeated chords in which Beethoven finally goes ONE-two-three, ONE-two-three, and gets us redirected both rhythmically and harmonically. Without that, it might have been impossible to find our way back. Part 7, in its entirety.

Musical example from Symphony No. 3 in E Flat Major, Op. 55, movement 1

And we're back. Without those repeated chords at the very end, we might not have been able to get back to a comfortable triple, and back we are. But when we come out of that part 7, I don't think we have any idea what to expect. It's like emerging from the fallout shelter in these 1950s movies, and wondering, "What will I see when I open that last door?"

George Grove wrote of this passage in 1896, "The hapless fugue is crushed by an outburst of rage, which forms the kernel of the whole movement, in which the most irreconcilable discords of the harmony and the most stubborn disarrangements of the rhythm unite to form a picture of obstinacy and fury, a tornado which would burst the breast of any but the most gigantic hero, whom Beethoven believes himself to be portraying and who is certainly more himself than Bonaparte."

The full development section, let us divide it into two parts, parts 1– 7, two large parts, and then part 8 through the conclusion, because we must deal with this awesome development, an earth-shaking, violently dramatic and moving development, filled with a level of contrast and pathos, the likes of which had never been heard, yet conceived, to its time. Part 1, the brief mysterious version of theme 1 heard at the end of the exposition is here extended. Part 2, theme 2, part 1, the lyric theme, returns quietly and lightly scored. This would seem to be not so bad; this won't be a tough development section. But quickly that gives way to part 3, theme 1, suddenly but quietly and very ominously, a minor mode sequence of theme 1.

Part 4, the action and drama explode. The theme 1 sequence continues to rise in the base, even as stirring descending hoofbeat motives gallop above. Part 5, theme 2, part 1, returns quietly, giving us a chance to catch our breaths and reorient ourselves before the next onslaught. Part 6, fugue, a dramatic minor-tinged fugue begins, its subject based on the hoofbeat rhythm, but just as this fugue starts to get off the ground, part 7 crashes in, and we go through that terrible experience of part 7. The dissociation, the struggle that it gives us, is extraordinary. Let us listen from part 1 through part 7, and we'll really hear 7 now as the core that it is. Development, part 1.

Musical example from Symphony No. 3 in E Flat Major, Op. 55, movement 1

Part 2.

Musical example from Symphony No. 3 in E Flat Major, Op. 55, movement 1

Part 3.

Musical example from Symphony No. 3 in E Flat Major, Op. 55, movement 1

Part 4.

Musical example from Symphony No. 3 in E Flat Major, Op. 55, movement 1

Part 5.

Musical example from Symphony No. 3 in E Flat Major, Op. 55, movement 1

Part 6.

Musical example from Symphony No. 3 in E Flat Major, Op. 55, movement 1

Part 7

Musical example from Symphony No. 3 in E Flat Major, Op. 55, movement 1

A lifeline.

Musical example from Symphony No. 3 in E Flat Major, Op. 55, movement 1

And now, we emerge from our shelter to see what's left of the countryside. Part 8, the so-called new theme, which is also sometimes called theme 6, a bittersweet song of pain and remembrance, scored for oboe and cello, represents well the blasted emotional landscape, and that new theme goes like this.

[Notes on piano]

This ostensibly new theme is in actuality a counter-theme, a theme that runs counter to our original theme 1, the triadic outline, so it's drawn from theme 1.

[Notes on piano]

That's theme 1. Let's just write a counter-melody to that base line.

[Notes on piano]

Indeed, our new theme is actually a counter-theme that's meant to fit at least subliminally with the triadic elements of theme 1, and so even it is related backwards to the opening of the piece.

Part 9, theme 1, triadic element, sequential development of the traffic elements of theme 1; part 10, a new theme, bittersweet melancholy theme, returns; part 11, a polyphonic sequence, a multi-melodied sequence, on theme 1 triadic element; part 12, disembodied harmonies and a single upward triad are all that remain. The music quiets. And then in the distance, a distant horn anticipates the entrance of theme 1 in the recapitulation.

Let us listen to development parts 8–12 and the beginning of the recapitulation, and be especially aware of how Beethoven brings everything down. Be very aware of that horn, which anticipates the beginning of theme 1, and then the unbelievable sense of satisfaction, arrival, and safety that come with the advent of the recapitulation, E flat major in theme 1 as originally heard. Development, part 8.

Musical example from Symphony No. 3 in E Flat Major, Op. 55, movement 1

Part 9.

Musical example from Symphony No. 3 in E Flat Major, Op. 55, movement 1

Part 10.

Musical example from Symphony No. 3 in E Flat Major, Op. 55, movement 1

Part 11.

Musical example from Symphony No. 3 in E Flat Major, Op. 55, movement 1

Part 12.

Musical example from Symphony No. 3 in E Flat Major, Op. 55, movement 1

Recapitulation.

Musical example from Symphony No. 3 in E Flat Major, Op. 55, movement 1

About that horn entry that anticipates the recap, Beethoven's student and friend Ferdinand Ries wrote: "In the first movement, Beethoven has a wicked trick for the horn. A few bars before the theme returns, Beethoven lets the horn anticipate the theme. For someone who is not familiar with the score, this always gives the impression that the horn player has counted wrong and has come in at the wrong place. During the first rehearsal of the symphony, which went appallingly, the horn player, however, came in correctly. I was standing next to Beethoven and, thinking it was wrong, I said, 'That damn poor player. Can't he count properly? It sounds infamously wrong.' I think I nearly had my ears boxed. Beethoven did not forgive me for some time."

Yes, Beethoven tended to take these things rather personally when someone got these wrong. Recapitulation, we're not going to listen to much of the recap, because much of the recap goes as we would expect it to, but one thing does not, and that is theme 1. I would read your WordScores of theme 1 of the recapitulation. "Measure 398, lyric majestic theme begins as it did in the exposition, but diverges soon enough. The dissonant chromatic step descent now continues downward past the C sharp to a C natural, instantly dispelling the darkness and tension that characterize the C sharp in the exposition."

Let me demonstrate this to you, because it's really great. The development section represents the struggle, and we have, for now, won that struggle. We've made it through the development section. What would be the point in dwelling on darkness and dissonance in theme 1 in the recapitulation if we've worked through these problems just now in the development? There would be no point, and so Beethoven does not dwell on dissonance here in theme 1. In the exposition, I would remind you, theme 1, phrase A, sounded like this.

[Notes on piano]

And implied that dark move to a minor key. But this is what happens in the recap.

[Notes on piano]

We suddenly find ourselves in the key of F major, not in the key of G minor, because…

[Notes on piano]

…Beethoven's step descent goes an extra step down, relieving instantly the negative tension, the dark energy of the exposition, and taking us to a very pleasant harmonic place. Please, let us listen to theme 1 in the recap, phrases A prime and A double prime.

Musical example from Symphony No. 3 in E Flat Major, Op. 55, movement 1

A prime.

Musical example from Symphony No. 3 in E Flat Major, Op. 55, movement 1

A double prime.

Musical example from Symphony No. 3 in E Flat Major, Op. 55, movement 1

Whether we notice or not, this is a very different theme 1. Let's talk about what's different between this version of theme 1 and what we heard in the exposition. First of all, we don't have the negativity implied by the C sharp which would resolve to G minor. Instead, the C sharp continues downwards. We go to F major, a very bright harmonic place as opposed to a dark harmonic. We do not have phrase B here in the recapitulation, with all its associated hemiolas and rhythmic dissonance. It's just not there. This has been purged in the music; we've dealt with all of this in the development section.

Instead, in phrase A prime, instead of a development of the opening phrase, we have a long and pleasant meander back from F major, which is where we've arrived because of the descending step motive, to A double prime, a marvelous and triumphant vision in E flat major of theme 1. This is a much more positive-sounding theme. It is missing the essential harmonic dissonance of C sharp leading to G minor and it's also missing the rhythmic dissonance of hemiola as represented by phrase B. That's neat. It's been purged; we've dealt with that already in the development section, and from here on out, the recapitulation acts pretty much as it should, bringing back the same materials we heard in the exposition, but now in the appropriate key areas, themes 2, 3, and the cadence material. So, I would draw our attention immediately to the coda.

Again, I quote George Grove: "Then comes a coda, 140 measures long, and so magnificently fresh and original as almost to throw all that has gone before it into the shade. The beginning of this coda is one of the most astonishing things in the whole of musical arts—and I will play it for you in a moment—and think what it must have been like in the year 1805, when even now, familiar as it is, after all that Beethoven himself has written since, all that Schubert, Mendelssohn, Schumann, Wagner, and Brahms, it still excites one's astonishment for its boldness and its poetry. This coda is no mere termination to a movement. Oh, no, it is an essential part of the poem and will be known as such. It is one of Beethoven's great inventions, and he knows it, and he starts it in such a style that no one can possibly overlook what he's doing."

Tell them, George. He's right on the button. Indeed, this gigantic coda is virtually a development of the development section in which darkness is banished and triumph reigns supreme. Part 1 of the coda is made to shock. Beethoven must do something to catch our attention, to galvanize us, that goes beyond anything he's done up to this point in the movement. That's hard to do. Beethoven would seem to have shown us every card his harmonic and rhythmic vocabulary can show. But he goes one step further. I read from your WordScore: "Coda, part 1, theme 1. Incredible and shocking downward sequence of theme 1, triadic opening, moves through the following keys: E flat major, D flat major, C major." Let me just play them for you first.

[Notes on piano]

That would be shocking for one of Beethoven's contemporaries because you don't go from E flat major to D flat major to C major like that. You just don't do that. You don't do that. We're used to so much stuff that we don't hear how shocking and brilliant those harmonic colors are, so, just the shock value, it's big. But there's something much more involved. Beethoven has harmonized a descending step descent of E flat.

[Notes on piano]

D flat

[Notes on piano]

C. This striking and, to his contemporary audience, outlandishly crude harmonic sequence, ties together the dissonance C sharp, which can also be spelled a D flat of the exposition.

[Notes on piano]

And the C natural that that descends to in the recapitulation.

[Notes on piano]

The alarming dynamic shifts that we hear accompanying these sequences of theme 1 also reinforce the harmonic shifts. But there's a metaphor here that's even more important, and I would discuss this now before we listen to the coda. The metaphor is, this phrase unites two things that, up to now, had been ununitable. It unites the heroic and broad triadic aspect of theme 1…

[Notes on piano]

…with the descending step descent that up to now has always been separate.

[Notes on piano]

But now he's harmonizing the triadic and heroic opening of the theme. He's harmonizing it with a bass line based on the step descent. This is very exciting, because it brings with it all kinds of metaphor. Light and dark aspects of the hero become one. This means self-awareness; the self is conquered; the self is understood. It's no longer separate parts of the personality, but the personality has absorbed everything. The bass line is the step descent; the melody is the triadic opening. They are mutually reinforcing, not fighting each other, but become one.

[Notes on piano]

It's a marvelous metaphor, and it's a metaphor that fits. Why would he have thought of it if this wasn't part of his thinking? It brings together all that has happened and makes it a singularity. Let's just listen to coda, part 1.

Musical example from Symphony No. 3 in E Flat Major, Op. 55, movement 1

45

Maybe in our world we're used to rather bloodier and more shocking things to shock us, but this should shock us. This should disrupt and disturb and at the same time fill us with a wonderful, effervescent glow, because, as I said, it unites something that up to now has been ununitable. The light and dark sides of the personality now become a single personality, now becomes self-awareness and control. The remainder of the coda is extraordinary, and it would seem to reflect this sense of the hero, its self-awareness and struggles won.

Part 2, the coda celebrates with increasing energy and joy—I'm not reading from your WordScores now, but my notes. The attainment of wholeness and self-awareness represented by part 1 of the coda inspires the music. Theme 1 sequence in second violins is accompanied by light and airy melody, derived from the fugue subject. Part 3, the new theme comes back and, yes, Beethoven has to bring the new theme of the development back somewhere. He can't bring it back in the recap, so he brings it back momentarily here, but just momentarily. This coda is about celebration; it's about newly obtained self- awareness and individual joy.

Part 4, light airy fugue subject derived from the development is heard again. Part 5, sequence of theme 1 motives in lower strings, rising wind motives, and violin tremolos created a bit of tense waiting using. Part 6, and now the celebration begins. Theme 1 in the horns as a now rising and prancing version of the hoofbeat motive would seem to describe victorious cavalry and parade. Measure 646, like a growing cheering crowd; more and more instruments join the parade. The texture thickens as intensity and excitement grows. Note the celebratory fanfares happening everywhere. Part 7, theme 2, part 2, gentle rising melody adds a measure of sweetness to the celebration. Part 8, a series of syncopated B flat 7 chords (that is, the dominant chord of E flat) creates one last hemiola, but it's not a threatening hemiola because the harmony is clear, and we know we are in E flat. A series of hammering B flat 7 chords lead to three detached E flat major tonic chords.

[Notes on piano]

Ending the movement as it began, the coda is a celebration. It's a celebration of the defeat of the dark side, which we witnessed in the development section, the emergence from part 7 of the development whole. The self-awareness gained through that experience is celebrated, and indeed in part 8 at the end of this coda we are in a magnificent and celebratory place. Let's listen to the coda and then draw our conclusions. Part 1.

Musical example from Symphony No. 3 in E Flat Major, Op. 55, movement 1

Part 2.

Musical example from Symphony No. 3 in E Flat Major, Op. 55, movement 1

Part 3.

Musical example from Symphony No. 3 in E Flat Major, Op. 55, movement 1

Part 4.

Musical example from Symphony No. 3 in E Flat Major, Op. 55, movement 1

Part 5.

Musical example from Symphony No. 3 in E Flat Major, Op. 55, movement 1

Part 6.

Musical example from Symphony No. 3 in E Flat Major, Op. 55, movement 1

Part 7.

Musical example from Symphony No. 3 in E Flat Major, Op. 55, movement 1

Part 8.

Musical example from Symphony No. 3 in E Flat Major, Op. 55, movement 1

By any measure, it is a remarkable movement, a remarkable bit of storytelling, a remarkable bit of composition. It's hard to believe, looking back, that the First Symphony, with all of its classicism and its careful developmental lines, was written only three years before this Third Symphony. Beethoven is a world apart from where he started, but we know that between the First Symphony and the Third has been the Heiligenstadt Testament, the coming to grips with the fact that his hearing is incurable and his maturing past the need to work within the classical style any longer, a revolutionary movement, but just the first movement of four extraordinary movements. We will return to movements 3 and 4 with Lectures Eleven and Twelve.

Lecture Eleven—Transcript
Symphony No. 3—The New Path—Heroism and Self-Expression, III

Welcome back to the symphonies of Beethoven. This is Lecture Eleven. We are continuing our four-lecture series on the Symphony No. 3 in E flat major, the "Eroica." And we will tackle movements 2, 3, and 4 in our next two lectures. But before we do, we've got to discuss Beethoven's mature compositional innovations, innovations which are pretty much in place as of the Third Symphony. These innovations comprise together what we would think of, what Beethoven spoke of, as his new path, innovations which collectively make the Third Symphony and Beethoven's music that follows the Third Symphony so different from the music that came before.

Compositional innovation number 1: Beethoven's post-Heiligenstadt Testament tenet that music must be above all a vehicle for self-expression. No single Beethovenian tenet, no single Beethovenian innovation, was more influential—because he was able to show what this new mode of expression could mean—than this great idea that music should be first and foremost self-expression, not decorative art, not something for the amusement of the cognoscenti or even the middle class, but the needs and feelings of the composer must always come first. This was very appealing to the 19th century that put individuality above all things, and continues to be the essential artistic tenet of the 20th century, self-expression—what do I want to say?—with the hopes that someone will want to hear.

Compositional innovation number 2: contextual use of form. Beethoven felt and said in his music that Classical Era forms can and should be altered, spindled, mutilated, folded, if necessary, to fit the dramatic context of a particular moment. Don't write a minuet and trio if something else is called for. Don't go right back to the first theme in the recapitulation in a certain key if something else is called for. Do what the context demands.

Mature innovation number 3: motific development as a unifying melodic compositional process. We have talked about this and will continue to talk about Beethoven's love of composing with small motific units and creating out of them ever greater tapestries of theme, all related back in a rhetorical logical fashion to a few earlier ideas.

Innovation number 4: rhythm. The elevation of rhythm and rhythmic manipulation, perhaps even devoid of melodic content, to a level equal to thematic and developmental music.

Five: dramatic progression of movements. Beethoven truly starts this concept with the Third Symphony, and that concept is as follows: The idea of the multi-movement symphony, not as four self-standing movements related as key but rather as a single constantly developing story line, like the multi-movement instrumental opera, with each movement playing another role in this large-scale story.

With these innovations in mind, innovations which we can track here in Symphony No. 3, let us proceed with movement No. 2, the Marche Fenebre, the Funeral March. The first question we have to ask is—really the question is—for whom does this bell toll? Is this movement about Napoleon? "I've come to bury Caesar, not to praise him." Well, not really. The composition of this movement far preceded Beethoven's rejection of Napoleon. According to Beethoven's friend and medical adviser, Dr. Andreas Bertolini, "The first idea for the 'Eroica' Symphony came to Beethoven from Bonaparte's expedition to Egypt. A rumor of Nelson's death in the battle of Trafalgar occasioned the funeral march." This was told to Bertolini by Otto John, an early Beethoven biographer in 1852, 49 years after the piece was written. I call this suspect info at best.

Is the funeral march written for the war dead? Perhaps, but we have to remember the great Napoleonic wars have not really started yet in 1803. So despite the fact that many have suggested it's about the war dead, I don't know. Perhaps the dramatic progression of movements is meant to mirror Beethoven's own life. Movement 1, we meet the hero and witness his courage in the face of fate. Movement 2, lapse into despair, caused by deafness—let's say a spiritual death, if not a physical one. Movement 3, the emergence from private hell via the life-enhancing energy of body rhythm. And movement 4, variations form symbolizing a new range of achievement and Promethean spirit.

Or perhaps the second movement funeral march is a necessary part of a more universal dramatic progression, less autobiographical. The first movement about heroic struggle, no individual person, but the concept of struggle; the second movement about death; the third movement about rebirth; the fourth movement about apotheosis. In the words of music historian Donald Grout, "Whatever the second movement funeral march might be about specifically, it addresses itself generally to the subject of heroism, sacrifice, and mourning."

Let's move immediately into the movement, the funeral march that begins without fanfare or introduction. I read from your WordScore: "A dismal and deeply pained theme set in the tragic key of C minor. The violins play the theme, but they are also told in the score sotto voce, which means under-voice, very suppressed and quiet." We hear this, as I said, in C minor, and I would ask you to note the somber drum rolls which are played by the contra basses, not by a drum. First we hear the theme in the violins, and then A prime, we hear it in an oboe.

Musical example from Symphony No. 3 in E Flat Major, Op. 55, movement 2

It's a real interesting feature of this theme, the fact that the drum roll is supplied first by the low strings and then by many more of the strings. One asks: Why didn't Beethoven simply use a drum? It's not a bad question, and the response is actually a little complicated. The kind of drum that is called for here is what's called a side drum, or a tenor drum. It's what we would see in the marching band played as the marchers proceed. Beethoven simply didn't have a drum like that or a drummer available to him in the orchestras of this time. If he had written this for timpani, No. 2, he might not have gotten the kind of sound he wanted, and, also, he wanted a sound with a clear pitch. He wanted a sound that would not only give the rhythm of drum but would give him the bass line that this music requires, and so he uses the strings instead. As long as they play cleanly, it will invoke both the drama and it will give him the clarity of bass line that he needs. That's why it's not drums. He didn't have a tenor drum available to him, and the timpani would not have worked for this purpose.

Beethoven's Marche Fenebre, this entire movement, more than any other movement in the Third Symphony, owes a clear debt to French Republican marching band models. For example, Francois Gossec: despite his bohemian name, he is a composer living and working in Paris. Gossec's Marche Lugubre (Lugubrious March; they had such lovely titles then) of 1790 displays many of the traits Beethoven borrows for his funeral march. For example, this Marche Lugubre, French march, uses dotted rhythms, muffled drum rolls, sobbing minor mode melody, half-step melodic motion, unison effects, and prominence given to the wind instruments.

I want to play you a little of Francois Gossec's Marche Lugubre of 1790, a French marching band march, and I want you to hear where Beethoven is coming from. Of course he would have heard this music, if not this particular piece, then music like this. Why would he have not heard it? He would have examined these scores, perhaps even heard this music in performance. This was contemporary music in Beethoven's day, and there's no reason why he shouldn't write a marching band piece along the models of a pre-existing genre. Let's listen just to the beginning of Gossec's march

Musical example from Gossec's Marche Lugubre

There's one point in Gossec's piece that sounds so much like a point in Beethoven's piece that one is almost tempted to draw a parallel, to say that Beethoven had heard the Gossec or was using aspects of it. I won't make that decision, but I'll let you make it on your own. I'll demonstrate at the piano this one passage I'm talking about. At one point in Gossec's march, we get this particular passage.

[Notes on piano]

And then at one point in Beethoven's funeral march, we get this passage.

[Notes on piano]

Boy, they sound a lot alike, and there are other such passages too. I really don't think Beethoven was stealing from Gossec—I don't think he needs to—but I think the genre of music gives itself to certain kinds of musical gestures. These descending gestures, these dotted rhythm harmonies, these very stentorian sounds, I think that is something in common between Beethoven and this French tradition, and that's what we're hearing in that resemblance.

Onward in Beethoven's piece, a piece then that clearly rose out of the pre-existing band tradition. The funeral march theme is continued; we'll pick up where we left off at measure 17. Following the dismal pained phrases of A and A Prime, which we've listened to, we hear a broad lyric melody, initially promising consolation and hope...

[Notes on piano]

…momentarily, in the much brighter key of the E flat major. This quickly gives way, however; the promising phrase lapses back to the tragic via a deeply moving and clearly operatic recitative, a recitation for cellos, the cello being the masculine voice of the hero, bringing us back to C minor. Let's pick up at measure 17 in part 1 of this movement, hear this consolation theme, which quickly draws back to C minor via this recitative-like line in the celli.

Musical example from Symphony No. 3 in E Flat Major, Op. 55, movement 2

The overall form of this movement features five large parts, and it is related to no particular pre-existing form. Beethoven is kind of making this up as he goes along. I'll just make the following generalizations about these parts. Part 1 features the funeral march, and we hear the funeral march two times. It's rather expository because we're hearing the main march. Part 2 features the redemption theme; that's the contrast, one moment of brightness in what is otherwise a rather dark and dismal movement. Part 3 brings the funeral march back again, but acts developmental; we get a fugue and some very interesting events. Part 4 is recapitulatory; we hear mostly funeral march, and part 5, a most remarkable coda. We're just going to taste little sections, pick and choose some parts. It's a very easy movement to follow. I don't feel the need to put the whole WordScore on the board for those of you who are watching. With WordScore in hand, this movement is easily followed. So, as I say, let's taste some moments.

Let's go directly to part 3, the funeral march development. Part 3 begins at measure 105, with a dismal and pained version of the funeral march, again in violins marked sotto voce. Let's get that back in our ear. Funeral March, part 3.

Musical example from Symphony No. 3 in E Flat Major, Op. 55, movement 2

But now, something very different happens. What happens is a fugue. A fugue is a Baroque Era procedure, usually an instrumental procedure (but not always) that features multiple voices, many different simultaneous melodies, usually the same melody, but overlapping itself in such a way as to create a thick and multi-melodied melodic surface. Just because the Baroque Era ends doesn't mean fugues don't keep being written. Beethoven wrote some of the great fugues of the Classical Era and indeed of the 19th century. We'll talk a lot more about fugue, especially when we get to the Ninth Symphony.

Something I mentioned in an earlier lecture that I would just bring back up for a moment. Beethoven studied between 1781 and 1792 with the court organist from Bonn, a gentleman named Neefe. Neefe, as I mentioned, was a Lutheran and someone very familiar with the music of Bach. It's a truism that Johann Sebastian Bach's music was essentially lost from the time of his death in 1750 until we get into the late 1820s. That is true. But the music that was lost or at least ignored tended to be Bach's big pieces, the big orchestral pieces, the concerti, the masses and so forth. The keyboard music stayed in currency, at least among pedants who were teaching their students how to play piano or harpsichord, and much of Bach's keyboard music kept being used by the cognoscenti, by the teachers. It wasn't publicly known, but certainly it was privately known.

Beethoven grew up playing Bach's keyboard music. He grew up playing preludes and fugues and probably also big organ pieces too. And Beethoven from the youngest age was awed by Bach and thrilled by Bach and adored the strict and absolutely clean polyphony multi-voiced writing of Bach's. The older Beethoven gets—it seems to be a truism with many people or composers, the older the composers get the less fluff they want, the more exactitude they seek. Beethoven found in Bach's fugues an amazing exactitude, an amazing spirit, an amazing expressive strength and power that he was drawn to as he got older and older, and so by the end of his life Beethoven isn't even looking at Haydn or Mozart anymore; he's looking at Bach, and he's looking very carefully at Bach, and he's writing these fabulous and extraordinarily moving fugues, sometimes to the point, like in his Op. 33, The Growth of Fugue, for string quartet, sometimes to the point where an entire composition is a fugal procedure. We shouldn't be surprised to find these baroque compositions in a Beethovenian context. Beethoven adored this music and was very familiar with it.

We get a fugue. Suddenly and starkly, this dramatic fugue bursts forth. The subject is based on an inversion of the broad lyric B of the funeral march. Remember that broad lyric B, that moment of consolation? It sounded like this

[Notes on piano]

We take that descending idea and we invert it. We just turn it upside down.

[Notes on piano]

And that becomes the new subject, an inversion of our lyric phrase B. It begins in the second violins, then the first violins come on, then the viola and the celli, and then the celli and the contra basses come in. Note also the accompanimental melody, the counter subject that goes with this fugue subject, gives the impression of tolling funeral bells. The fugue builds in intensity with rapid staccato scales sounding like raindrops falling on the cortège. Finally, the polyphony, all of these many voices, and this is one of Beethoven's favorite games, the polyphony solidifies into a series of vicious and dissonant C sharp diminished chords. Yes, they sound like this…

[Notes on piano]

…which only, after wreaking havoc on our souls, resolve to an open cadence clearly aimed toward G minor. Here's what I want you to listen for now, the strength of this fugue, the dismal mood, and this trick that Beethoven will indulge in more and more, and which I'll point out as it occurs over the course of this course, taking the many voices of a polyphonic setting and suddenly allowing them to congeal into huge and powerful harmonies. It's just something he's going to do and something we should be aware of. Fugue, which occurs in part 3 of the funeral march.

Musical example from Symphony No. 3 in E Flat Major, Op. 55, movement 2

I find a level of expression, a level of feeling here that's really hard to describe. This is not someone affecting a funeral march. Whatever emotion Beethoven was putting into this piece, and this becomes a very difficult thing to talk about, emotion and expression and feeling, because one person's feeling is another person's gobbledygook, but there's tremendous power here; there is a great amount of sincerity in this music. Beethoven is writing from experience, and the darkness that pervades the music is not a put-on. There really is a tremendous sense of pathos here for my ear, and it only becomes more powerful in the passage that follows. Immediately after the fugue ends, we hear a brief version of the funeral march. It is a pathetic and forlorn version that is suddenly left hanging on the pitch A flat. The march is so bereft, it's so filled with despair, that it cannot even complete itself, but rather chokes up on this pitch.

[Notes on piano]

Very quiet in the violins. Suddenly, all the low strings grasp that A flat and play it viciously.

[Notes on piano]

And then add to that A flat a full A flat measure triad…

[Notes on piano]

…which, if you think sounds pretty, it does not. It is shocking in all the strings. Stark, massive fanfares in the brass strike like a terrifying vision of final judgment. Built on this A flat, it came out of nowhere, and we really just jump into this terrifying moment, which finally resolves downwards…

[Notes on piano]

…to a G chord, which resolves…

[Notes on piano]

…back to C minor in part 4. Part 4 begins with a funeral march in the oboe and the clarinet, and I would point out, note the heavy syncopated accompanimental figure that imbues this passage with a plodding, shuffling, distraught weight.

[Notes on piano]

What we're going to hear is this pathetic and forlorn version of the funeral march that follows the fugue, the hang-up on A flat, the grasping of A flat by the low strings, the A flat major chord that follows, and then the stark, funereal fanfares, the vision of judgment played by the brass, followed by this shuffling and plodding version of the funeral march.

Musical example from Symphony No. 3 in E Flat Major, Op. 55, movement 2

Part 4.

Musical example from Symphony No. 3 in E Flat Major, Op. 55, movement 2

I don't want to lead anyone to a suicidal edge, so I think it's necessary for us to visit part 2, the redemption theme, and see at least what a little bit of hope feels like in this otherwise despairing landscape, so let's take a look at part 2, the redemption theme, a necessary and lovely contrast. Part 2 from your WordScores: "Upwards-reaching melody, accompanied by gentle triplets, suggests a ray of light amid the despairing gloomy darkness." Note the low strings play an accompaniment pattern derived from the drum roll. The drum roll had gone like this.

[Notes on piano]

Now, they simply slow that down and play this.

[Notes on piano]

And, again, it's something that's built on the past, but in the present it sounds different, so Beethoven creates a sense of unity between the funeral march and the redemption theme, yet we might not notice on the surface how unified they are because they sound different enough to sound different, yet they're unified enough to be unified, very slick, very nice. At measure 76, an almost victorious sounding tremolo chord on a G tremolo means that the string players are asked to go back and forth very quickly with their bow hand on a single pitch, and it creates a shivering sense of excitement, and then the redemption theme resumes at measure 80, and that's as much as we'll listen to. Just a taste, just a sense of what this theme sounds like. Part 2, measure 69, redemption theme.

Musical example from Symphony No. 3 in E Flat Major, Op. 55, movement 2

This is pretty much it; this is our respite in an otherwise dark and dismal movement. By the way, this peaceful and beautiful music returns just once, and that is in the coda, so let's look forward to the coda. It is a coda in three parts, and it is what I'm calling part 5 in the piece. I would read from your WordScores, and we're going to pick this up at measure 200, which is actually immediately before part 5 where the coda begins. At measure 200, we have essentially, as in part 1, that is, a brief codetta, a brief concluding section, which leads to this cadence in C minor.

[Notes on piano]

But instead of resolving back to C minor...

[Notes on piano]

…that cadence is going to deceptively cadence, which means this.

[Notes on piano]

We call that a deceptive cadence. That's when the chord of tension, the dominant chord, resolves somewhere other than where we expected it to. In this case, it resolves to an A flat major chord, the same A flat chord that we heard back in part 3, at that moment of final judgment. The deceptive cadence suddenly and unexpectedly redirects the music to A flat major, and that brings us into part 5 on the coda. Extraordinary and beautiful, we are momentarily transported to a gentle twilight world before the inevitable return to earth and the reality of death.

Coda, part 1, starts with clocklike ticking in the strings, almost the time of our lives ticking away. Measure 213, the redemption theme returns, beatific, almost childlike variant of the theme, it's at once wistful and filled with sadness and melancholy. It is exquisitely beautiful. This move back to C minor, part 2, the redemption theme variant, breaks apart. Ashes to ashes, dust to dust, a staccato flute moves downward, and lastly, part 3, the funeral march, in an anguished fragmented version, demonstrates well the pained eloquence of silence as it virtually disintegrates beneath our ears. Let's listen to this final bit of the movement, starting in measure 200, which is the concluding section of part 4, and then all of part 5.

Musical example from Symphony No. 3 in E Flat Major, Op. 55, movement 2

Deceptive cadence.

Musical example from Symphony No. 3 in E Flat Major, Op. 55, movement 2

Part 5.

Musical example from Symphony No. 3 in E Flat Major, Op. 55, movement 2

Part 1 of Part 5.

Musical example from Symphony No. 3 in E Flat Major, Op. 55, movement 2

Redemption theme.

Musical example from Symphony No. 3 in E Flat Major, Op. 55, movement 2

Part 2.

Musical example from Symphony No. 3 in E Flat Major, Op. 55, movement 2

Part 3.

Musical example from Symphony No. 3 in E Flat Major, Op. 55, movement 2

Deeply felt, very dark, it's time to bring us out of this funk, back to the daylight, but before, an anecdote told by George Grove in his book on the Beethoven symphonies. An interesting anecdote is told about the Symphony during the first few months of its existence, of which even the accurate Thayer (Thayer being an early Beethoven biographer) sees no reason to doubt the truth. Prince Luis Ferdinand of Prussia, a remarkable musician and composer, whose piano playing Beethoven placed above even that of Hummel, and whom the great composer complimented as "not playing at all like a royal person, but like a real musician," was on a visit to Prince Lobkowitz in early 1805 at his castle at Raudnitz in Bohemia. Desiring especially to honor his illustrious guest, Lobkowitz arranged for a performance of the new symphony by his orchestra, which always attended him.

The two princes took their seats, and the great work was played straight through. Luis Ferdinand listened with the utmost interest, and at the close of the performance, entreated for a repetition of the entire symphony, which immediately took place. He was then so fascinated as to beg for a third on the ground of his departure early the next morning. "Willingly," said Lobkowitz. "if we may first give the band some dinner." The dinner was accordingly given, the two princes (let us hope) taking part in it with the players, and then the immortal symphony was once more played over. Three times in one night, I'm not sure who was working harder, the listeners or the musicians.

In any case, I would quote Grove one more time: "It is impossible to imagine a more complete relief than the scherzo provides after the funeral march." Scherzo allegro vivaci, fast and with life. Introduction, I read from your WordScores: "The introduction sets a playful elfin mood, with six measure of quiet staccato chattering in the strings. Measure 7, the scherzo theme, the theme itself is a frisky, quirky tune, which opens with B flat repeated seven times."

[Notes on piano]

Just wanted to make sure I had done that seven times and not eight, but I did. We hear that theme twice in the oboe. Let's just listen to measures 1–30, the introduction and the first appearance of the scherzo theme in this third movement, and, remember, this immediately follows that dismal and heartfelt ending we just witnessed in the Funeral March.

Musical example from Symphony No. 3 in E Flat Major, Op. 55, movement 3

Relief is rife; it's as if we've just gotten some adrenaline pumped right into our hearts. The sky has opened back up again, the roof has come off the hall, and the light has come flooding back in. Please, let me read through the remainder of the scherzo on the WordScore, and then listen to this entire scherzo section. "We should call this scherzo a melody in search of a tonic, that is, a tune in search of a tonal basis with which it's comfortable," because Beethoven starts scooting through so many keys there's a sense of mercurial movement that does not get anchored until well into this movement.

"At measure 31, introductory chattering, longer than before, the key changes, then we hear the scherzo theme on the flute in F. major." That's not good enough. "The strings imitate the last portion of the theme, and then introductory chattering begins again. The key changes again. The texture reduces to a single B flat, which is repeated a whole bunch of times in the low strings, then more introductory chattering. The scherzo theme is heard, this time in B flat major." We're getting close to E flat; we're getting close to the ostensible tonic of this movement, and finally at measure 93, the scherzo theme extended and celebratory, everybody at E flat major. We made it, the darkness has completely passed, and a marvelous thing happens.

Phrase B at measure 115, two exuberant descending E flat major arpeggios, celebrate the arrival finally in E flat major, and I'll point out the syncopations after we've had a chance to hear this music. Then at 127, the introductory chattering begins again, and we move towards our closing cadence. We will hear the scherzo from beginning to end, twice. Beethoven is indicated it is to be repeated, and we will hear that repetition. So again, here, I'll help you out. This is where we were at the end of the second movement.

[Notes on piano]

Scherzo, third movement.

Musical example from Symphony No. 3 in E Flat Major, Op. 55, movement 3

Back.

Musical example from Symphony No. 3 in E Flat Major, Op. 55, movement 3

Measure 41.

Musical example from Symphony No. 3 in E Flat Major, Op. 55, movement 3

56.

Musical example from Symphony No. 3 in E Flat Major, Op. 55, movement 3

73.

Musical example from Symphony No. 3 in E Flat Major, Op. 55, movement 3

85.

Musical example from Symphony No. 3 in E Flat Major, Op. 55, movement 3

93.

Musical example from Symphony No. 3 in E Flat Major, Op. 55, movement 3

115.

Musical example from Symphony No. 3 in E Flat Major, Op. 55, movement 3

And the scherzo comes to its conclusion, and we have been uplifted to a place that is so far beyond the second movement it's hard to imagine such an emotional transition in such a brief period of time. I want to spend a couple of seconds pointing out that phrase B again, those exuberant arpeggios that celebrate the arrival to E flat major, because we will recognize phrase B. If I just play it at the piano, it goes like this.

[Notes on piano]

Syncopated one-TWO-THREE, one-TWO-THREE. But of course, if we just listen to the pitches.

[Notes on piano]

Comes right out of the first movement. That's no mistake, and mistakes like this can't possibly happen. And so it's a celebration of heroism; it's a celebration of arrival; it's a celebration of wholeness, and the syncopations do not give it ambiguity so much as great and visceral excitement. Let's listen. Phrase B.

Musical example from Symphony No. 3 in E Flat Major, Op. 55, movement 3

The only point I'm going to point out in scherzo 2, and this will bring this lecture to its conclusion, and we'll pick up in the trio in our final lecture of the symphony, is this scherzo da capo; that is, when the scherzo comes back later, it comes back pretty much as we just heard it, with one huge difference, and that's what happens with Phrase B; it's a fabulous difference. When we get to phrase B, in the second scherzo, in the da capo, I read from your WordScore, "As in scherzo 1, the first time we hear that arpeggio, an exuberant descending E flat major arpeggio celebrates E flat major." Note the syncopations, but here's what's different at measure 381. Beethoven tells us *alla breve*, cut time. Unlike scherzo 1, the second E flat major arpeggio is played in duple meter, a most exhilarating and surprising turn of events. Let's just listen to that once, talk about it one more time, and listen to it again. Scherzo da capo, 372.

Musical example from Symphony No. 3 in E Flat Major, Op. 55, movement 3

381.

Musical example from Symphony No. 3 in E Flat Major, Op. 55, movement 3

What Beethoven does is change meter on us. Hadn't this been implied all through the first movement, which was also in triple meter, with all those hemiolas, acting like he was in duple meter, just for a moment, and switching back to three? Here he has syncopations one-TWO-THREE, one-TWO-THREE, one-TWO-THREE, and then he does the one thing that he never really did in the first movement, simply change meter. ONE-two, ONE-two, ONE-two. And he does: in the score, he actually goes from triple meter to duple meter. It's a shocking and wonderful moment, and we should absolutely be aware of it. It's a smile, it's a big smile whenever we hear this piece. Again.

Musical example from Symphony No. 3 in E Flat Major, Op. 55, movement 3

And so forth, and so on, very exhilarating, again, Beethoven using rhythm and rhythmic manipulation to create great sense of dramatic narrative development and great exhilaration. With that exhilaration ringing in our ears, let us take our lecture break. When we return, we will talk about the trio, a marvelous and terrifying solo for horns, and move on to the brilliant and controversial fourth movement.

Lecture Twelve—Transcript
Symphony No. 3—The New Path—Heroism and Self-Expression, IV

Welcome back to the symphonies of Beethoven. This is Lecture Twelve, the fourth and last lecture dealing with Beethoven's Symphony No. 3, the "Eroica," and I pick up immediately from where I last left off, and that was at the trio of the third movement scherzo. I read from your WordScores: "Trio, a true trio, this passage is scored for three horns with some wind and string interjections. This is in E flat major."

By the way, I must provide this note for you. Beethoven provides few if any dynamic indications for the horns; that is, he's not telling the horns how soft or loud to play their solo. Beethoven is going to be overjoyed no matter what the horns give him. As long as the horns can play the darned pitches, Beethoven's happy. Play them loud, play them soft, just play them. A brief moment to discuss the horn as an instrument. Mothers, don't let your children grow up to be horn players. It is by far the most difficult, the most unforgiving instrument anyone has ever invented. It's almost an instrument of sado-machismo—to inflict it on the child and to play it. It has a tiny little mouthpiece into which one has to spit with unbelievable force to create even the most flatulent sound. To play a horn in tune, to play it well, is almost impossible, and in Beethoven's day they didn't have the nicety of those valves on the horns to help find the pitches. They had to overblow into higher octaves in order to get what we call the chromatic tones in these natural unvalved horns. So you bet Beethoven's going to be very happy to get whatever the horn players can do. Ask them to play soft or loud? Just play my pitches, please. I would tell you that horn players, still to this day, grow nauseous at the thought of playing the dizzy ascent which constitutes phrase C.

Let me read us through the rest of the trio, and then we will listen to the trio in its entirety. "Phrase B, simple, almost rustic phrase features a long-short rhythm. A quiet and slow descent leads us to C Prime horn with tutti interjections, ending, the trio does, with a quiet extension leading to a glowing twilight mood at trio's end, a sort of twilight mood rare in this symphony. Please note that phrases D and C prime are repeated. Beethoven Symphony No. 3, scherzo trio. Let's listen.

Musical example from Symphony No. 3 in E Flat Major, Op. 55, movement 3

Phrase B.

Musical example from Symphony No. 3 in E Flat Major, Op. 55, movement 3

C Prime.

Musical example from Symphony No. 3 in E Flat Major, Op. 55, movement 3

Phrase D.

Musical example from Symphony No. 3 in E Flat Major, Op. 55, movement 3

C Prime.

Musical example from Symphony No. 3 in E Flat Major, Op. 55, movement 3

And then, of course, we head out to scherzo 2. Much to my great pleasure, we have enough time to play this entire movement, and that's what we will do. You'll forgive me for speaking over the performance, but I will indicate the measure number where we are at any given moment, so that those following with WordScores can keep track. It's up to you, as I've said before and as I will undoubtedly say again, it's up to you to go out, spend those extra few bucks on recordings of the Beethoven symphonies if you haven't already, which I imagine most of you have, and then follow without the annoying intrusion of my voice, your WordScores with just the music. For our purposes, I will provide that extra little service. Beethoven's Symphony No. 3, third movement scherzo, which comes, as we've said, with incredible relief after the dark, dank despair of the Funeral March.

Musical example from Symphony No. 3 in E Flat Major, Op. 55, movement 3

Measure 7.

Musical example from Symphony No. 3 in E Flat Major, Op. 55, movement 3

41.

Musical example from Symphony No. 3 in E Flat Major, Op. 55, movement 3

56.

Musical example from Symphony No. 3 in E Flat Major, Op. 55, movement 3

73.

Musical example from Symphony No. 3 in E Flat Major, Op. 55, movement 3

85.

Musical example from Symphony No. 3 in E Flat Major, Op. 55, movement 3

93.

Musical example from Symphony No. 3 in E Flat Major, Op. 55, movement 3

115.

Musical example from Symphony No. 3 in E Flat Major, Op. 55, movement 3

127.

Musical example from Symphony No. 3 in E Flat Major, Op. 55, movement 3

Repeat.

Musical example from Symphony No. 3 in E Flat Major, Op. 55, movement 3

41.

Musical example from Symphony No. 3 in E Flat Major, Op. 55, movement 3

73.

Musical example from Symphony No. 3 in E Flat Major, Op. 55, movement 3

85.

Musical example from Symphony No. 3 in E Flat Major, Op. 55, movement 3

93.

Musical example from Symphony No. 3 in E Flat Major, Op. 55, movement 3

115.

Musical example from Symphony No. 3 in E Flat Major, Op. 55, movement 3

127.

Musical example from Symphony No. 3 in E Flat Major, Op. 55, movement 3

Trio.

Musical example from Symphony No. 3 in E Flat Major, Op. 55, movement 3

D.

Musical example from Symphony No. 3 in E Flat Major, Op. 55, movement 3

C prime.

Musical example from Symphony No. 3 in E Flat Major, Op. 55, movement 3

Repeat D.

Musical example from Symphony No. 3 in E Flat Major, Op. 55, movement 3

C prime.

Musical example from Symphony No. 3 in E Flat Major, Op. 55, movement 3

Scherzo da capo.

Musical example from Symphony No. 3 in E Flat Major, Op. 55, movement 3

265.

Musical example from Symphony No. 3 in E Flat Major, Op. 55, movement 3

299.

Musical example from Symphony No. 3 in E Flat Major, Op. 55, movement 3

315.

Musical example from Symphony No. 3 in E Flat Major, Op. 55, movement 3

343.

Musical example from Symphony No. 3 in E Flat Major, Op. 55, movement 3

351.

Musical example from Symphony No. 3 in E Flat Major, Op. 55, movement 3

373.

Musical example from Symphony No. 3 in E Flat Major, Op. 55, movement 3

385.

Musical example from Symphony No. 3 in E Flat Major, Op. 55, movement 3

Coda.

Musical example from Symphony No. 3 in E Flat Major, Op. 55, movement 3

It is an explosive and celebratory conclusion, a world away from the way we ended the second movement in that dark, dismal, and dank place just moments ago. Movement 4, a true curiosity: Up to this point, I've described the fourth movement in metaphoric terms, as an apotheosis, as a variations form movement that symbolizes a new range of achievement, a compositional rebirth, a fecundity of frankly effervescent mock ferocity imbued with a Promethean spirit. If all of this is true, and how can it not be—after all, this is our serious Beethoven; this is our wild-haired madman of musical seriousness— then how do we explain the following commentary contained in George Grove's book on the Beethoven symphonies?

"The finale is a puzzle. Some have thought it trivial, some labored, others that its intention was to divert the audience after too long a strain of the earlier movements. 'The Symphonia "Eroica" of Beethoven,' wrote the best English musical writer of his day on a performance in April of 1827, 'most properly should end with the funeral march, omitting the third and fourth movements, which are entirely inconsistent with the avowed design of the symphony.' We might surely have more confidence in Beethoven's genius, and in the results of the care and consideration he applied to both the design and details of his works."

Indeed, Beethoven attached the following note to the first editions of both the score and parts of the Third Symphony. Beethoven's note: "This symphony, being purposely written at greater length than usual (understatement city) should be played nearer the beginning than the end of the concert, or shortly after an overture, an air, or a concerto, lest it is heard too late for the audience when fatigued by the previous pieces. It should lose its proper and intended effect." What Beethoven is saying is, please program this symphony up front, because if you program it near the rear end of a program—and programs were longer in Beethoven's day—there's no chance the audience will keep up. There's an amusing tribute to the length of this piece. It comes to us from the first public performance in 1805, where Karl Czerny, Beethoven's student and friend, heard someone say, "I'd give a kreuzer if the damn thing would stop!" Yes, the symphony is rather long by 1805 standards, which brings us back to the question at hand. Is the fourth movement a sublime apotheosis or is it a marvelous comic relief?

Please remember that, traditionally, fourth movements of Classical Era symphonies were intended to be fast, frisky, and upbeat. My advice while listening to this movement is twofold. First, I think we should approach it with the same sense of fun that Beethoven had while composing it, and, two, toss out forever any notions associated with the word "Eroica." Movement 4 of the music, introduction, I read from your WordScores: "Dramatic downwards rushing strings, followed by an explosive fanfarish cadence. This grand, magnificent, introductory music must surely signal an event of singular import. G minor leading to a huge, open cadence." Let's listen to this, please.

Musical example from Symphony No. 3 in E Flat Major, Op. 55, movement 4

If that was not a ta-da, I don't know what is a ta-da. And now for something extremely important: What follows this huge and all-embracing introduction? This.

Musical example from Symphony No. 3 in E Flat Major, Op. 55, movement 4

Huh? Ta-da? This is it? After all of that fuss, a silly, mousy little tune emerges, resembling a tippy-toed little dance. We were prepared for a king, and instead we get a clown. And I call this the bass theme. We hear the bass theme once and then again, clownish tippy-toed theme heard again, this time answered by out-of-step winds. What can Beethoven possibly be up to? This is very comic, indeed, burlesque music.

Again I read from your WordScores the following analysis—that is, my discussion—of measures 28–43, with great thanks to the English commentator Antony Hopkins, who wrote, "Abnormal music demands an abnormal approach." Donald Tovey wrote of this following passage, "It is quite absurd, and we can almost see Beethoven laughing in our mystified faces." Hopkins again: "The really disconcerting thing about this passage is not its humor but its slapstick humor." Indeed, let's take a look at the WordScores and talk about this next passage, these measures 28–43, and you will excuse me if I kind of narrate with them. First, I will simply play them at the piano. We have a silence at measure 28 that followed that tippy-toed, out-of-kilter dialogue between the bass theme and the winds.

[Notes on piano]

What can this possibly mean? This is very theatric music, and I will suggest a very theatric interpretation, irreverence be damned. So far it's the strings who've play this silly little clownish tune, so we should think of the strings as the clowns (that's rather apt, a piano player saying that) but, okay, the strings are the clowns. So what happens after a silence is that the winds, brass, and percussion, the rest of the orchestra, cannot believe what they've heard. This is the best you can do? So the winds, brass, and orchestras say, "Knock, knock, knock, wake up."

[Notes on piano]

Silence, because no one responds, and then they say it again.

[Notes on piano]

Meanwhile the bass theme, the clownish strings, resume. "Did you hear something?" "No, I didn't hear nothing."

[Notes on piano]

Another silence. The rest of the orchestra is getting really peeved at this point. Then suddenly, the strings say, "Did someone say knock, knock, knock?

[Notes on piano]

And the winds, brass and percussion say, "You bet we did."

[Notes on piano]

The strings say, "Oh."

[Notes on piano]

"Got a problem with that?" say the winds, brass, and percussion. The strings say, "Oh, no," and so they finish their little tippy-toed dance.

[Notes on piano]

It's silly, it is silly, it is burlesque, but it's what Beethoven wrote. We can't make this any different from what it is, and that's what it is. So let us listen from the beginning of the movement, that huge introduction, the introduction to the bass theme, that silly, mousy little nothing, big deal, and then that marvelous dialogue between the rest of the orchestra and the strings, as the rest of the orchestra tries to figure out, "Is this all you're gonna do?" and the bass theme says, "Yeah, this is who I am." Measure 1–43.

Musical example from Symphony No. 3 in E Flat Major, Op. 55, movement 4

Think about what you just heard. Is this any way to begin a symphonic movement, especially one that purports to belong in a symphony entitled "Eroica"? Since its creation, commentators have attempted to reconcile this comic, this burlesque fourth movement with the power, depth, and solemnity of movements 1 and 2. And it gets worse before it gets better. I would read from your WordScores at measures 44–75: "The bass theme takes a crack at thematic respectability. It realizes the rest of the orchestra doesn't seem to have the proper respect for it." It's been dissed, and it needs to restore some sense of face, so it clothes itself in proper phrase structure and accessorizes with harmonic and melodic accompaniments. Yes, now we hear an AA, BA, BA, and then an AA, BA, BA. It tries to act like a real theme with real phrases and real harmonies, but ask yourself while listening to this extension of the bass theme whether this sounds both satisfactory and substantial.

Musical example from Symphony No. 3 in E Flat Major, Op. 55, movement 4

Repeat.

Musical example from Symphony No. 3 in E Flat Major, Op. 55, movement 4

B.

Musical example from Symphony No. 3 in E Flat Major, Op. 55, movement 4

A prime.

Musical example from Symphony No. 3 in E Flat Major, Op. 55, movement 4

B.

Musical example from Symphony No. 3 in E Flat Major, Op. 55, movement 4

A prime.

Musical example from Symphony No. 3 in E Flat Major, Op. 55, movement 4

Measure 60.

Musical example from Symphony No. 3 in E Flat Major, Op. 55, movement 4

Repeat.

Musical example from Symphony No. 3 in E Flat Major, Op. 55, movement 4

B.

Musical example from Symphony No. 3 in E Flat Major, Op. 55, movement 4

A prime.

Musical example from Symphony No. 3 in E Flat Major, Op. 55, movement 4

Repeat B.

Musical example from Symphony No. 3 in E Flat Major, Op. 55, movement 4

Having asked yourselves those questions of substance and satisfaction, I think this theme comes up short indeed. Do we really buy this bass theme stuff? It would seem that this movement has yet to get off the ground. Do we really believe this clownish theme can continue to carry the movement? What's going on? Finally, at measure 76, the master theme comes home, the truth be known, an explanation. The boss is back. The truth is revealed, the bass theme is not a theme at all, but a bass line for an infinitely more memorable master theme. If this is our bass theme…

[Notes on piano]

…it really is a bass line under this much more interesting theme.

[Notes on piano]

And so forth. Yes, it is a servant that has been parading around in the master's clothes while the master was out doing its master theme things somewhere else. At measure 84, note the knock, knock, knock in accompaniment, and now we hear an entire theme. The master, the A, A prime, B, A double prime, B, A double prime, and now the music finally sounds like it's starting, and we chuckle, because we realize everything up to this point has been a slight of hand, this bass theme parading around as if it owned the place, when all along master was simply out. Let's listen to the master theme, please.

Musical example from Symphony No. 3 in E Flat Major, Op. 55, movement 4

A prime.

Musical example from Symphony No. 3 in E Flat Major, Op. 55, movement 4

B.

Musical example from Symphony No. 3 in E Flat Major, Op. 55, movement 4

A double prime.

Musical example from Symphony No. 3 in E Flat Major, Op. 55, movement 4

B.

Musical example from Symphony No. 3 in E Flat Major, Op. 55, movement 4

A double prime.

Musical example from Symphony No. 3 in E Flat Major, Op. 55, movement 4

So it is a bass line, and it's a good bass line, that bass line is, but it's a silly, mousy little melody if it's heard all by itself. This fraud, this impostor, this servant in master's clothes, has been revealed.

Beethoven loved this tandem; he used it twice. He used it in the finale of the Prometheus ballet, Op. 43 of 1801, and he used this tandem as the theme for his piano variations, Op. 35 of 1802, so it's a melodic duality that appealed to him very much. But never before did he use it with a sort of comic setup and development as he does here in the Third Symphony. Our game plan for the remainder of the movement: the master theme returns periodically, each time somewhat varied. Alternating with these appearances of the master theme are episodes in which the bass theme tries to reassert its dominance over the movement, only to be humorously brushed aside by the various returns of the master theme.

For example, I read from your WordScores and measures 107–206. "At 107, we have a brief interlude transition, which would seem to augur, finally, some rather more serious developments and an open cadence." Then the bass-themed fugue—oh indeed, the master theme has gone out again, and the base theme tries to take over. That clownish wacky bass theme, the servant in master's clothes, refuses to accept its accompanimental place in the musical scheme. Here the bass theme initiates what seems to be at first a serious and substantial fugue. Indeed, it starts in the first violins, in the second violins, the violas, the cellos, and the basses, and it even starts sounding heroic.

But, suddenly, the master theme comes home in variation 1. We harmonized in minor at first; the quick modulation to major unfairly obliterates the serious self-important mood of the bass-themed fugue. Indeed, the master theme continues, light playful phrase in flutes and oboes, with chattering violin accompaniment. That's A prime, phrase

B, brilliant highly embellished passage for solo flute, as we listen to the master theme variation 1. It's so humorous, it's so light, it's so brilliant, that it absolutely obliterates whatever heaviness the bass theme tried to generate by acting self-important in the fugue. Let's pick it up at measure 107 during the interlude; we'll hear the bass-themed fugue and the master theme come home once again.

Musical example from Symphony No. 3 in E Flat Major, Op. 55, movement 4

From the master theme.

Musical example from Symphony No. 3 in E Flat Major, Op. 55, movement 4

107, interlude.

Musical example from Symphony No. 3 in E Flat Major, Op. 55, movement 4

Bass-themed fugue.

Musical example from Symphony No. 3 in E Flat Major, Op. 55, movement 4

Master theme returns.

Musical example from Symphony No. 3 in E Flat Major, Op. 55, movement 4

A prime.

Musical example from Symphony No. 3 in E Flat Major, Op. 55, movement 4

B.

Musical example from Symphony No. 3 in E Flat Major, Op. 55, movement 4

B prime.

Musical example from Symphony No. 3 in E Flat Major, Op. 55, movement 4

A.

Musical example from Symphony No. 3 in E Flat Major, Op. 55, movement 4

Do we feel how this movement is going? The bass theme takes over, tries to get serious; the master theme comes back and blows away the seriousness, its musical ego utterly flattened, its balloon punctured, its parade rained upon, derided, mocked, and, worst of all, giggled at, sniggled at, snorted at. The bass theme is too stupid to give up. Let's pick up at measure 207. Another brief interlude transition paves the way for another bass theme episode. This is the bass theme march, the bass theme in low strings under a serious-sounding march in C minor. Is this finally Napoleon? It's doubtful; it's really hard to take this movement very seriously at this point. Antony Hopkins suggests toy soldiers at the Battle of Bakerloo, General Whosis vs. Field Marshal Whatshisname.

First, we'll hear the bass theme in the bass under the march tune, and then the bass theme will go into the top voice into the soprano. A loud, fussy cadence ends this bass theme march, and we would think that this music had become serious, but, no, again, the master theme comes back. Variation 2, just phrase A, absolutely comic intrusion, the master theme again deflates the pretensions of the bass theme with a light and playful appearance, back and forth, back and forth. Really, these contrasts are so broad they become comic, and comic they are. Let's pick it up from the last B prime of the master theme, variation 1; that would be measure 199. Then we'll move into the interlude, the bass theme march, and the master theme, variation 2.

Musical example from Symphony No. 3 in E Flat Major, Op. 55, movement 4

Interlude.

Musical example from Symphony No. 3 in E Flat Major, Op. 55, movement 4

Bass theme march.

Musical example from Symphony No. 3 in E Flat Major, Op. 55, movement 4

Big fussy cadence.

Musical example from Symphony No. 3 in E Flat Major, Op. 55, movement 4

Oh, stop it, take those clothes off and go clean the windows! Yet, it really is utterly dismissive and very common. Like it or not, we've got to respect that bass theme's moxie. At measure 266, after that little bit of variation 2 that we just heard, the master theme finally and fully acknowledges the bass theme in a wonderful double fugue. Again, I'm throwing these terms—fugue and double fugue—around a good bit. Let me backtrack and explain again.

We talked about fugue apropos of the second movement, funeral march. We talked about the fact that it was a genre of polyphonic or contrapuntal music that was perfected during the high baroque period, particularly by composers like Handel and especially Johann Sebastian Bach. It is a procedure that, while not used as often as it would have been used in the baroque, and not quite with the strictness of baroque fugues, it's a procedure that lives on even into modern music. Beethoven is a master of fugue, he's a master of Bach's music and increasingly, as he gets older, he does look to Bach models for composing, and this includes Bach's fugues.

We have a lot of fugues in the Third Symphony. We have a lot of complex polyphonic music, although albeit classical complexity, that is, Classical Era themes that are much more vocal and lyric than Baroque Era themes might have been. Nevertheless, Beethoven is giving us another fugue, and this one is a double fugue. A double fugue is a fugue that does not have just one fugue subject, that is, overlapped with itself and various accompanimental melodies. Double fugue is one with two subjects, two main themes heard simultaneously, which are then accompanied by various overlapping versions of themselves and other accompanimental melodies. Fugues are hard enough to write; if you're teaching fugue, as I have taught, you can get your students to writing passable fugues, if you start in September, by January. But double fugues, coming up with two fugue subjects that work with themselves, each other, and other melodies? Oh no, double fugues are not easy to write at all. And they're not easy to project these independent voices.

Beethoven does it beautifully; we already know that the bass theme and the master theme will work in tandem when necessary, and so he allows them to work in tandem, but now accompanied by many other overlapping versions of themselves and other accompanimental melodies. What this does, metaphorically of course, is render for a moment the bass theme equal to the masters theme, because in a double fugue, each subject, each melody would be of equal importance, and that's what we hear.

I read from the WordScore: "Master theme, bass theme, fugue. This fugue utilizes both the master theme and the bass theme. It begins quietly and mysteriously, but soon builds to a large exciting proportion." It starts just master theme and bass theme and builds and builds and builds. I put a note in your WordScores, which I would read: "Through all the ever-building polyphonic complexity of this fugue, there is a good-natured humor here, a lightness and playfulness that betrays the academic seriousness of what we often think a fugue is." At measure 346, the polyphony solidifies into the same sort of fanfarish harmonies that closed the introduction, and, again, Beethoven is doing here in the fourth movement what he did in the second movement: bringing all the complex and multiple polyphonic lines ultimately together, congealing them (coagulating them, if you will) into a more singular homophonic texture, one where there's one main melody and everything else accompanimental, so all the diverse parts kind of overlap and then merge into a more singular musical texture. It's a very nice way of bringing this theme to its conclusion, and it's something that Beethoven likes to do. So, let us listen to the double fugue of the bass theme and the master theme from measures 258. We're going to pick up with the master theme variation 2, and then shoot right into this master bass theme fugue. On we go.

Musical example from Symphony No. 3 in E Flat Major, Op. 55, movement 4

By giving it equal time in this marvelous double fugue, the bass theme is finally satisfied. It's been paid respect to, it's been used in a principal melodic way, along with its ostensible master, and it is satisfied enough to bow out gracefully and will not rise again to the surface for the remainder of this movement, happy from here on out to simply play an accompanimental role, having been accepted and respected as it was.

Let's move forward then. I will read from your WordScore at measure 349: "Master theme and variations 3 and 4. Variation 3: poco andante." Beethoven asks the orchestra and conductor to slow things down, a little andante, a little walking speed, con expressione, with expansion. A gorgeous lyric and innocent version of the master theme, we hear phrase A in the wind choir, phrase A prime played by strings, phrases B and A prime embellished—note the rolling clarinet in the accompaniment, and further embellished in the last two phrases, B and A prime.

We will listen straight through to the master theme variation 4, a magnificent and regal setting. Note the wind-brass fanfares and the triplet violin accompaniment. We hear it at first in phrase A in the low strings, clarinets, bassoons, and horns, a very rich and thick musical timbre, very powerful, very profound. Again, if one is looking too hard for Napoleon, one might look to this master theme variation 4, but it's too late to find Napoleon; Napoleon's not here. This is just a very beautiful theme that Beethoven is deciding now to do in a number of variations so that he can fully explore all of its possibilities. We've had its puckish possibilities, its humorous possibilities, now its lyric possibilities in variation 3, and its magnificent possibilities in variation 4. Let's listen to the master theme variations 3 and 4.

Musical example from Symphony No. 3 in E Flat Major, Op. 55, movement 4

A prime.

Musical example from Symphony No. 3 in E Flat Major, Op. 55, movement 4

B.

Musical example from Symphony No. 3 in E Flat Major, Op. 55, movement 4

A prime.

Musical example from Symphony No. 3 in E Flat Major, Op. 55, movement 4

B.

Musical example from Symphony No. 3 in E Flat Major, Op. 55, movement 4

A prime.

Musical example from Symphony No. 3 in E Flat Major, Op. 55, movement 4

Variation 4.

Musical example from Symphony No. 3 in E Flat Major, Op. 55, movement 4

B.

Musical example from Symphony No. 3 in E Flat Major, Op. 55, movement 4

A Prime.

Musical example from Symphony No. 3 in E Flat Major, Op. 55, movement 4

Finally, I would point out that we get a chunk of music, this variation 4, royal and magnificent, that is deserving of the introduction that began this movement. After all the intervening material, we finally got to something that would stand up to the ta-da. And now it's time to bring the symphony to its conclusion, coda in six parts. Lengthy, as befits this magnificent symphony, it first winds us down and then ratchets us all into the stratosphere. I would read your WordScore: "Part 1, gentle triadic motives," which are very reminiscent of:

[Notes on piano]

From the first movement, alternate with staccato strings: Part 2, the master theme, almost another variation, though the theme is embellished and syncopated, and as such difficult to pick out; Part 3, master theme hidden in syncopated first violins; part 4, the introduction comes back, dramatic downward rushing strings from the opening of the movement—now the intro does indeed lead to something exciting; part 5, in horns, the master theme, sounding just like hunting music, blares forth; and part 6, E flat major scales, arpeggios and chords, chords and more chords. A thrilling and extended E flat major conclusion caps the symphony, a huge expansion of how the symphony began.

[Notes on piano]

Here at the conclusion about 55 minutes later, let us listen and then draw our final conclusions. Coda.

Musical example from Symphony No. 3 in E Flat Major, Op. 55, movement 4

Part 2.

Musical example from Symphony No. 3 in E Flat Major, Op. 55, movement 4

Part 3.

Musical example from Symphony No. 3 in E Flat Major, Op. 55, movement 4

Part 4.

Musical example from Symphony No. 3 in E Flat Major, Op. 55, movement 4

Part 5.

Musical example from Symphony No. 3 in E Flat Major, Op. 55, movement 4

Part 6.

Musical example from Symphony No. 3 in E Flat Major, Op. 55, movement 4

In the summer of 1817, 14 years after its composition, poet Christian Kuffner was dining (after the composition of the Third Symphony) with Beethoven in Nussdorf at the inn Zur Rose. Kuffner asks Beethoven, "Tell me, frankly, which is your favorite among your symphonies," at which time Beethoven had composed the first eight. Beethoven's response: "The 'Eroica.'" Kuffner: "I would have thought the C minor," meaning No. 5. Beethoven: "No no, no no, the 'Eroica.'" And why not? It's a cutting-edge piece of great artistic courage, closely associated with Beethoven's own coming of compositional age, as well as his coming of emotional age, a piece on which Beethoven built the whole of his subsequent output.

MOVEMENT I *Sonata-Allegro form*
"Allegro con brio (♩ .= 60)" triple meter (3/4)

Exposition

"Introduction"
More like a
harmonic "preface;"
two riveting tonic
Eb Major chords
establish both tonic
Eb and a powerfully
macho mood

tutti

Theme 1
A theme of stunning motivic, harmonic and
rhythmic complexity and expressive breadth.
Theme 1 personifies the "hero," and its motives ◢

Phrase *a*: A theme of lyric majesty emerges,
consisting of 2 essential motivic ideas — a
broad, triadic (Eb Major) opening followed
by an incredible and "dissonant" chromatic
step descent from Eb – D – C#:

etc.

⌞ triadic/ ⌟ ⌞ step descent ⌟
harmonic
element ***a***

Note: Descent to C# (and subsequent upwards resolution
to "D") momentarily darkens the harmony and adds a
huge degree of emotional complexity (a dark side!) to
our hero

Note also: Initial appearance of this broad, lyric theme in
orchestral cellos immediately establishes a rich,
masculine persona

23

Phrase *b*: The triadic element of the theme,
isolated and extended in phrase *a'*, is now further developed; it is inverted and elongated:

To this falling motive a new element is added: rhythmic disruption
via hemiola:

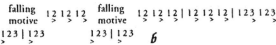

falling	1 2 1 2 1 2	falling	1 2 1 2 1 2	1 2 1 2 1 2	1 2 3 1 2 3
motive	> > >	motive	> > >	> > >	> >
1 2 3	1 2 3		1 2 3	1 2 3	***b***
>	>		>	>	

etc.

Note: Hemiola also creates a march meter (duple)
in this otherwise triple meter movement!

will sire all the other themes in the movement. As a result, the other themes are not so much "contrasts" as they are different facets of the same rich personality: **Theme 1**

15

Phrase a¹: Once the key of E♭ Major has been reattained, Beethoven immediately begins extending/developing various aspects of the theme; this phrase sees the <u>triadic element</u> of the theme isolated and sequenced upwards:

a ¹

37

Phrase a²: Triumphant and magnificent, the heroic theme celebrates, via the <u>triadic element</u>, the reattainment of the downbeat and with it, rhythmic stability

a ²

ff

<u>Note</u>: There is no step descent and no "C♯"-like dissonance here to "cloud" this victorious music

Theme 2: Spawned from the <u>step descent</u> of **Theme 1**

<u>45</u>

Part 1: Gentle, lyric theme appears directly out of the end of **Theme 1**, without any intervening bridge passage; the theme consists of a series of light-as-a-feather 3-note descents derived from the <u>step descent</u> of **Theme 1**:

Vigorous orchestral unison descent (based itself on the <u>step descent</u>) spans a 6th

 etc.

ff

<u>Note</u>: Each subsequent statement of the motive marks an intervallic expansion (development) over the previous version of the motive

B♭ Major
p

ff

<u>65</u>

Transitional Passage
Behaves like the modulating bridge we never had!

Part 1: Stirring descending "hoofbeat" motives: ♪♫♫♪ lead the transitional charge

Part 2: Roiling sweeping strings lead to

Vigorous orchestral unison descent (now spanning over 2 octaves!)

modulatory ⟶
f

ff

↘

<u>103</u>

The momentarily quiet, gentle respite is over; staccato, stepwise strings initiate a rapidly developing transition ⟶

cresc. - - - - - -

<u>109</u>

Cadence Material
Part 1: <u>Cadence Theme</u>; spawned from the triadic element of **Theme 1**; triumphant, heroic, triadic theme has, despite the triple meter, a distinctly martial/march-like character:

 etc.
f *sf* *sf* *sf* *ff*

B♭ Major

<u>Note</u> the <u>syncopations</u> — they will soon be the downfall of this strutting, macho music!

Part 2: The vigorous orchestral descent (itself an outgrowth of the **Theme 1** <u>step descent</u>) is inverted to create a gentle, rising melody:

Music
quickly
becomes
dramatic
and
animated

Bᵇ Major

84

Theme 3

Spawned from the triadic/harmonic element of **Theme 1**. Tender, harmonically conceived theme made up of repeated, triadically ascending harmonies:

99

The groups of 3
repeated chords
gives way to
groups of 2!

| ♩ ♩ ♩ | ♩ ♩ ♩ | etc.

pp

Bᵇ Major

119

Part 2: Fiery strings play a rising sequence; note the hemiola: the rhythm is being significantly disrupted!

ff

1 2 3 | 1 2 3 | 1 2 3 | 1 2 3
  >   >   >   >   >
(1 2 1   2 1 2   1 2 1   2 1 2)
  >   >   >   >   >

123

Part 3: The music tries to "right" itself with a 3-note <u>step descent</u>

ff

It doesn't work! The music breaks down into a series of 2-chord descending units

| ♩ ♩ ♩ | etc.

4x total

85

(Cadence Material, cont.)

128

Yikes! The 2-chord units break down into a single chord, heard in hemiola:

1 2 1 2 1 2 1 2 1 2 1 2
  >   >   >   >   >   >

C$\frac{6}{4}$

132

Part 4: Rising, triadic motive from **Theme 1** saves the day!

sf *p* $\longleftarrow$ *ff*

144

Falling arpeggios (triads) of 3 notes each (**Theme 1**)

3x total

f

Pedal "B♭" $\longrightarrow$

Development

An earthshaking, violently dramatic and moving development, filled with a level of contrast and pathos, the likes of which had never been heard (yet conceived!) to its time

152

Part 1: The brief, mysterious version of **Theme 1** heard at the end of the **Exposition** is here extended, dissipating the energy and B♭ Major mood of the **Exposition**

pp

166

Part 2: Theme 2, Part 1 returns, quietly and lightly scored

"dolce"

C Major

p

(Now, this isn't so bad! This is kind of nice!)

220

Part 5: Theme 2, Part 1 returns quietly, giving us a chance to catch our breaths and reorient ourselves before the next onslaught

A♭ Major

p

236

Part 6: Fugue

A dramatic, minor-tinged fugue begins, its subject based on the "hoofbeat" rhythm ♫♫ of Part 4; HOWEVER, just as the fugue is getting "off the ground" …

p   *cresc.* - - - - - - - - - - - -

147

Huge, tutti, dissonant A°7 chords (vii°7 of B♭) heard over the pedal "B♭"; They are a grim equivalent to the opening two E♭ chords

ff

➤

148

Part 5: Brief, mysterious version of <u>Theme 1</u> opening

B♭ Major

p

178

Part 3: <u>Theme 1</u> Uh-oh; suddenly but quietly (and very ominously), a minor-mode sequence of the <u>Theme 1</u> opening appears, accompanied by shivering tremolos in the strings

Theme 1 sequence:		Theme 1 sequence:	
1st x	2nd x	3rd x	4th x
c minor	c♯ minor	d minor	e minor
pp	*p* < *ff*	*ff*	

186

Part 4: The action and drama explode! The <u>Theme 1</u> sequence continues to rise in the bass even as stirring, descending "hoofbeat" motives ♫♫ gallop above

Quiet, nervous arpeggios	Theme 1 sequence:		Quiet, nervous arpeggios, extend.
	5th x	6th x	
	g minor	a minor	
p < *ff*		*ff*	*p f ff*

248

Part 7: Development part from hell! The fugue — a dark enough bit of music in its own right — is brutally cut off by this genuinely brutal music! This incredible passage — filled with dissonance, modal ambiguity and rhythmic ambiguity (hemiolas!) — represents the abyss and forms the dramatic core of the movement

ff

A series of crisp repeated chords acts like a lifeline in a stormy sea; meter and tonality are re-established and we wait to see what, if anything, has survived the onslaught!

B7

87

| 284 |

Part 8: "New Theme"
A bittersweet song of pain and remembrance,
scored for oboe and cello, represents well the
blasted emotional landscape:

e minor

p

| 300 |

Part 9: Theme 1,
triadic element;
sequential development
of triadic element of
Theme 1

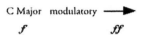

C Major   modulatory ⟶

f   *ff*

This ostensibly "new theme" is in actuality a
counterpoint to the triadic element of **Theme 1**:

Recapitulation

| 396 |

Introduction
Two magnificent,
triumphant B♭7 chords
(V of E♭) explode
from the orchestra; the
hero is back and would
seem to have survived
the **Development** intact!

f   *ff*

| 398 |

Theme 1
Lyric, majestic theme begins as it did in the
Exposition but diverges soon enough — the
dissonant chromatic step descent now continues
downward to C♮, instantly dispelling the darkness
and tension that characterized the C♯ in the
Exposition

a

E♭ Major   modulatory ➤

©1998 The Teaching Company.

322	**338**	**382**

Part 10:
"New Theme"
Bittersweet, melan-
choly theme returns

clarinet/   flute/
bassoon   violin/
                       cello

e♭ minor   G♭ Major

p

Part 11:
Polyphonic
sequence on
Theme 1
<u>triadic</u>
<u>element</u>

modulatory →

p < *ff*

Part 12:
Disembodied
harmonies
and a single,
upwards triad
are all that
remain; the
music quiets

f > *pp*

Quiet string
tremolos

<u>Note</u>: Distant
horn
anticipates
the entrance
of **Theme 1**
in the
Recapitulation

pp

408

The downward move to the C♮
results in a key change, which
in turn provides Beethoven
with the opportunity to create
an extended, modulatory
phrase within the thematic
recapitulation!

Triumphant
and magnificent
version of
Theme 1

(<u>Note</u>: The
rhythmically
troubled,
hemiola-filled
phrase **b** does
<u>not</u> appear in the
recapitulation of
Theme 1)

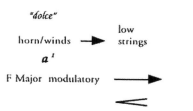

"*dolce*"

horn/winds →   low
                         strings

a¹

F Major modulatory ──────→

<

tutti

a²

E♭ Major

f < *ff*

Theme 2
Spawned from the step descent of __Theme 1__

Part 1: Gentle, lyric theme grows directly out of the end of __Theme 1__, consists of a series of 3-note descents

E♭ Major

p

Vigorous orchestral unison descent spans a 6th

ff

460

Part 2: Inverts the vigorous orchestral unison to create a gentle, rising, step-wise melody

E♭ Major

p   <

486

Theme 3
Spawned from the triadic/harmonic element of __Theme 1__

Tender theme made up of repeated, triadically ascending harmonies

E♭ Major

p

Groups of 3 repeated chords gives way to groups of 2:

| ♪ ♩ ♩ | ♪ ♩ ♩ | etc.

Strings initiate an energetic transition

cresc. - - - - - - - -

527

It doesn't work! The music breaks down into a series of 2-chord descending units

4x total

Yikes! The 2-chord units break down into single chords, heard in hemiola

F$^6_5$

535

Part 4: Rising triadic motive from __Theme 1__

p < *ff*

| 468 |

Transitional Passage

Part 1: Stirring,
descending
"hoofbeat" motives

Part 2: Roiling,
sweeping scales

Part 3: Vigorous
orchestral unison descent

modulatory ⟶

f

ff

| 511 | | 521 | | 526 |

Cadence Material

Part 1: <u>Cadence Theme</u>
Spawned from the triadic element
of <u>Theme 1</u>; triumphant, heroic,
triadic theme; note syncopations

Part 2: Fiery
strings play a
rising sequence
marked by
hemiola

Part 3: The
music tries to
"right" itself
with a 3-note
step descent

Eᵇ Major

f

ff

| 547 | | 550 | | 551 |

Three falling
arpeggios
(triads) of 3
notes each

Huge, tutti, dissonant D°⁶₅
(vii°⁶₅ of Eᵇ) chords heard
over pedal "Eᵇ"; equivalent
to the movement opening 2
chords

Part 5: <u>Very</u>
brief, mysterious
version of <u>Theme
1</u> opening

f

ff

p

Pedal "Eᵇ" ⟶

Coda

A development of the **Development**; darkness is banished and triumph reigns victorious

> 553

Part 1: <u>Theme 1</u>

Incredible and shocking downward sequence of <u>Theme 1</u> triadic opening moves through the following keys: Eb Major, Db Major, C Major; Beethoven has "harmonized" a step descent of Eb – Db – C! This striking and, to his contemporary audience, outlandishly crude harmonic sequence ties together the dissonant "C#" ("Db") of <u>Theme 1</u> in the **Exposition** with the C♮ of <u>Theme 1</u> in the **Recapitulation**

Alarming dynamic shifts accentuate the impact of the alarming harmonic shifts:

Eb Major	Db Major	C Major
p $>$ pp	f p	$f\!f$ p

> 595

Part 4: Light, airy, fugue-subject derived accompaniment moves to the fore-front; heard in a sequence

p

> 603

Part 5: Sequence of <u>Theme 1</u> motives in lower strings, rising wind motives and violin tremolos create a bit of tense, waiting music

pp

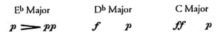

Pedal "Bb"

> 623

Gentle, descending motives in the flute and violins dispel completely any residual tension!

p

> 673

Part 7: <u>Theme 2</u>, Part 2

Gentle, rising melody adds a measure of sweetness to the celebration

Eb Major

p *cresc.* - - - - -

> 681

Part 8: A series of syncopated, tutti Bb7 chords (V7 of Eb) create one last hemiola:

|123|123| 123 |123|123|
  >   >   >   > >   >

$f\!f$ (|2| 2|2)   <u>Note</u>: One
                >   >   >   last "march"!

567

Part 2: <u>Theme 1</u> sequence in 2nd violins is accompanied by a light and airy melody derived from the fugue subject:

581

Part 3: "New Theme" from the **Development** reappears for what is a necessary thematic "recapitulation"

winds/low strings

f minor   modulatory   ➔

p

631

Part 6: <u>Theme 1</u> in the horns as a now rising, prancing version of the "hoofbeat" motive would seem to describe victorious cavalry in parade:

etc.

E♭ Major

p

646

Like a growing, cheering crowd, more and more instruments join the parade; the texture thickens as intensity and excitement grow!

<u>Note</u>: Celebratory fanfares in trumpets and timpani, which eventually move to all the brass ➔

cresc. - - - - - - - - *ff*

Series of hammering B♭7 chords

ff

Three detached E♭ Major tonic chords end the movement as it began

ff

MOVEMENT II

"March funebre. Adagio assai (♪ = 80)" duple meter (2/4)

Part One

<u>Funeral March</u>
A dismal and deeply pained theme set in the "tragic"
key of c minor

"Drum roll"
motive moves
into all strings

violins, "*sotto voce*"
a
c minor

<u>Note</u>: Sombre "drum
roles" — ♫ ♪ — are
supplied by the contrabasses

oboe

a¹

p < >

31

<u>Funeral March</u> resumes

1st violins
a
f minor

p < *f p*

Lyric phrase

winds
b
E♭ Major   modulatory ⟶

p < *f p* < >

"Drum roll"
motive in strings

Part Two

69

Redemption Theme
Upward reaching melody, accompanied
by gentle triplets, suggests a ray of light
amid the despairing, gloomy darkness

C Major

cresc. - - - - - -

<u>Note</u>: Low strings
play an accompani-
ment pattern derived
from the "drum
roll" motive:

"drum roll"

new accomp.

76

Almost
victorious
sounding
tremolo
chord

G Major

ff

©1998 The Teaching Company.

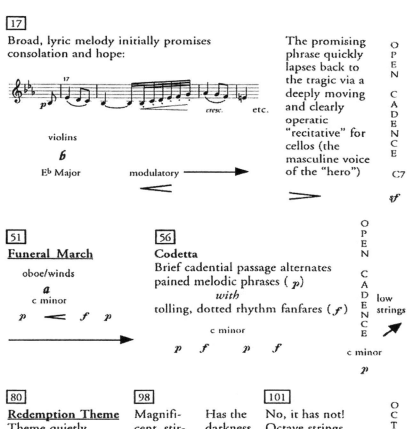

17

Broad, lyric melody initially promises
consolation and hope:

violins

b

Eb Major   modulatory ⟶

The promising
phrase quickly
lapses back to
the tragic via a
deeply moving
and clearly
operatic
"recitative" for
cellos (the
masculine voice
of the "hero")

O
P
E
N

C
A
D
E
N
C
E

C7

sf

51

Funeral March

oboe/winds

a

c minor

p ◁ *f* *p*

⟶

56

Codetta
Brief cadential passage alternates
pained melodic phrases (*p*)
       with
tolling, dotted rhythm fanfares (*f*)

c minor

p *f* *p* *f*

O
P
E
N

C
A
D
E
N
C
E

low
strings

↗

c minor

p

80

Redemption Theme
Theme quietly
resumes, ultimately
building up to ...

violins   winds
F Major C major

p   *p* cresc. ---- *ff*

98

Magnifi-
cent, stir-
ring and
most vic-
torious
sounding
tremolo
chord
C Major

Has the
darkness
been
conquer-
ed?

101

No, it has not!
Octave strings
slowly descend, out-
lining the Neapol-
itan (bII) of c minor;
darkness falls across
the music almost
instantly!

f p

O
C
T
A
V
E

"B's"

O C
P A
E D.
N

p

Part Three

105

Funeral March
Dismal and
pained

violins, "*sotto voce*"

a

c minor

p

114

Fugue: Suddenly and starkly, this
dramatic fugue bursts forth; the subject
is based on an inversion of the broad,
lyric "*b*" of the __Funeral March__:

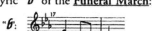

"*b*:

Fugue
subject:

1st v ⟶
2nd v ⟶
f
va/vc ⟶
vc/cb ⟶

__Note__:
Ringing,
slow-
moving
counter-
subject
gives the
impression
of tolling,
funeral
bells

The fugue
builds in
intensity,
with rapid,
staccato
scales
sounding
like
"raindrops
falling on the
cortège"
(Hopkins)

Part Four

173

Funeral March
Dismal, plodding and pained!

oboe/clarinet

a

c minor

p

__Note__: Heavy syncopated accompanimental
figure imbues this passage with a plodding, shuffling,
distraught weight:

181

Broad, lyric melody
initially promises
consolation

violins

b

E♭ Major

p

"Drum roll"
motive in
strings
destroys the
hope of the
opening and
darkens the
passage

c minor

Part Five: Coda

Extraordinary and beautiful; we are momentarily transported to a gentle twilight world
before the inevitable return to earth and the reality of death

209

Part 1: Starts with
clocklike "ticking" in
the strings

A♭ Major

f   decresc. - - - -   *p*

213

Redemption Theme
Beatific, almost childlike
variant of the theme is at once
wistful and filled with sadness
and melancholy

A♭ Major

p

Modulates
back to c
minor via
Neapolitan

(D♭)

150

The polyphony solidifies into a series of vicious and dissonant C#o7 chords

ff

O
P
E
N

C
A
D
E
N
C
E

D7

154

Funeral March

Brief version left hanging on a pathetic and forlorn "Ab"

violins
a¹
g minor
p

158

Stunning, melodramatic attack on the Neapolitan of g minor

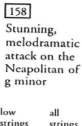

low strings	all strings
unison "Ab's"	Ab Major chord
ff	*ff*

160

Stark, massive fanfares in brass strike like a terrifying vision of final judgment

(The "Ab" eventually falls to "G," the V of c minor)

ff >

Tragic cello recitative, heard among "drum roll" motives brings a return to ...

195

oboes/clarinets
a
f minor
p < >

200

Codetta
Essentially as in **Part One** until ...

c minor

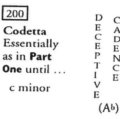

D   C
E   A
C   D
E   E
P   N
T   C
I   E
V
E

(Ab)
f

The deceptive cadence suddenly and unexpectedly redirects the music to Ab Major!

223

Part 2: The **Redemption Theme** variant breaks apart

c minor

Staccato flute/ violin descent

238

Part 3: **Funeral March**
Anguished, fragmented version demonstrates well the pained eloquence of silence

c minor
pp

f > *p*

MOVEMENT III

"Scherzo. Allegro vivace (♩. = 116)" triple meter (3/4)

Scherzo

Introduction
The introduction sets a playful, elfin mood with 6 measures of quiet staccato "chattering" in the strings

Eb Major
pp

[7]
Scherzo Theme
The theme itself is a frisky, quirky tune which opens with "Bb" repeated seven times:

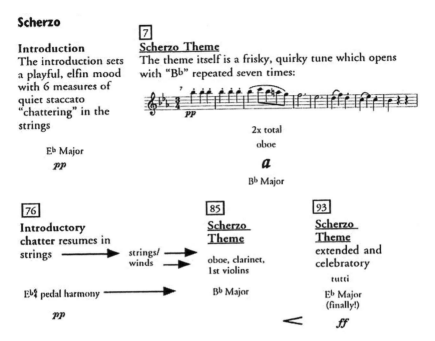

2x total
oboe

a

Bb Major

[76]
Introductory chatter resumes in strings ➡ strings/ ➡
winds ➡

Eb⁶₄ pedal harmony ⸺⸺⸺➡
pp

[85]
Scherzo Theme

oboe, clarinet, 1st violins

Bb Major

[93]
Scherzo Theme extended and celebratory

tutti

Eb Major (finally!)

< *ff*

Trio

[167]
A true "trio," this passage is scored for <u>3 horns</u> (with wind/string interjections):

c

Eb Major

<u>Note</u>: Beethoven provides few dynamic indications for the horns; he would have been happy for them to "simply" play the correct pitches and rhythms!

Coming on the heels of the funeral march, this scherzo
provides the most stunning contrast imaginable

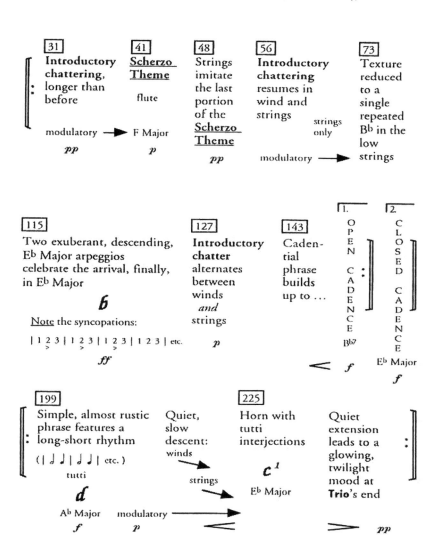

31	41	48	56	73
Introductory chattering, longer than before	**Scherzo Theme** flute	Strings imitate the last portion of the **Scherzo Theme**	**Introductory chattering** resumes in wind and strings *strings only*	Texture reduced to a single repeated B♭ in the low strings
modulatory ➔ F Major				
pp	*p*	*pp*	modulatory ➔	

115	127	143	⌐1.	⌐2.
Two exuberant, descending, E♭ Major arpeggios celebrate the arrival, finally, in E♭ Major	**Introductory chatter** alternates between winds *and* strings	Caden-tial phrase builds up to ...	OPEN CADENCE	CLOSED CADENCE
b				
Note the syncopations:			B♭7	E♭ Major
| 1 2 3 | 1 2 3 | 1 2 3 | 1 2 3 | etc.	*p*			
ff		< *f*		*f*

199		225	
Simple, almost rustic phrase features a long-short rhythm (| ♩ ♪ | ♪ ♪ | etc.)	Quiet, slow descent: winds	Horn with tutti interjections	Quiet extension leads to a glowing, twilight mood at **Trio**'s end
tutti			
d	strings	***c¹***	
A♭ Major	modulatory ➔	E♭ Major	
f	*p*		*pp*

©1998 The Teaching Company.

99

Scherzo

255	265	287	299	306
Introductory chatter	<u>Scherzo Theme</u> Heard 2x in oboe	Introductory chatter	<u>Scherzo Theme</u> flute	Strings imitate the last portion of the <u>Scherzo Theme</u>
modulatory ➡	B♭ Major	modulatory ➡	F Major	
pp	*p*	*pp*	*p*	

343	351	373
<u>Scherzo Theme</u>	<u>Scherzo Theme</u> Extended and celebratory	As in first **Scherzo**, an exuberant, descending E♭ Major arpeggio celebrates E♭ major
oboe/ clarinet	tutti	Note syncopations:
B♭ Major	E♭ Major	
p <	*ff*	

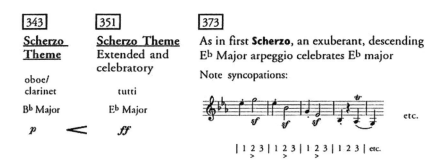

| 1 2 3 | 1 2 3 | 1 2 3 | 1 2 3 | etc.

etc.

385	401	
Introductory chatter alternates between winds *and* strings	Cadential phrase builds up to ...	O P E N C A D E N C E B♭
p	< *ff*	P A U S E

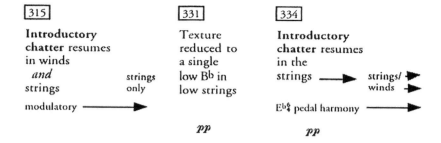

315		331	334	
Introductory chatter resumes in winds *and* strings	strings only	Texture reduced to a single low Bb in low strings	**Introductory chatter** resumes in the strings ⟶	strings/ ➤ winds ➤
modulatory ⟶			Eb$^6_4$ pedal harmony ⟶	
		pp	*pp*	

315 | strings only

331 | **Texture** reduced to a single low Bb in low strings — *pp*

334 | **Introductory chatter** resumes in the strings ⟶ strings/winds

Eb$^6_4$ pedal harmony ⟶ — *pp*

| 381 |

"Alla breve (o = 116)"
Unlike first **Scherzo**, the 2nd Eb arpeggio is played in duple meter — a most exhilarating and surprising turn of events!

Coda
Brief!

| 423 |

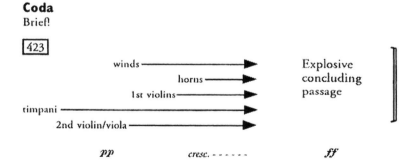

winds ⟶
horns ⟶
1st violins ⟶
timpani ⟶
2nd violin/viola ⟶

Explosive concluding passage

pp   *cresc.* - - - - - -   *ff*

MOVEMENT IV

"Finale, Allegro molto ($\quad$ = 76)" duple meter (2/4)

Introduction
Dramatic, downwards rushing strings
followed by an explosive, fanfarish
cadence; this grand, magnificent
introductory music must surely signal
an event of singular import!!!

g minor   modulatory ———————▶

ff

O
P
E
N
C
A
D
E
N
C
E

P
A
U
S
E

B♭7

TA-DA!!!

20

Bass Theme
Clownish, tippy-
toe theme heard
again, this time
answered by out-
of-step winds

pizz. strings

E♭ Major

Note: The following "analysis" with thanks to
English commentator Antony Hopkins, who wrote
"abnormal music demands an abnormal approach"

Donald Tovey wrote of this passage: "[It] is quite
absurd, and we can almost see Beethoven laughing in
our mystified faces ..."

Hopkins again: "The really disconcerting thing about
[this passage] is not its humor, but its slapstick humor."

28

S
I
L
E
N
C
E

36

Strings (arco): "Did
someone say
Knock
    Knock
        Knock!?!?"
in octave "B♭'s"

ff

Winds, brass and percussion:
Knock
    Knock
        Knock!
in octave "B♭'s"
("You got a problem with
that?)"   *ff*

Strings:
"No
problem!"

"B♭'s"
p

12

Bass Theme

Ta-da? This is it? After all that fuss? A silly, mousy little tune emerges, resembling a tippy-toe little dance! We were prepared for a king, and instead we get a clown:

pizz. strings
Eᵇ Major
p

29

Winds, brass
and percussion:
Knock
Knock
Knock!
in octave "Bᵇ's"
ff

30

S
I
L
E
N
C
E

31

Winds, brass
and percussion:

⌒

sustained
"Bᵇ's"
p

Bass Theme
Clownish strings:
"Is someone
there?"
They resume
their tippy-toe
theme
Eᵇ Major
p

P
A
U
S
E

Winds,
brass and
percussion:
"Good!"

⌒

"Bᵇ's"
p

40

Bass Theme
Strings and
winds resume
their out-of-
step version of
the clownish
theme
p

(Exit stage left!)

Note: Is this any way to begin a symphonic movement, especially one that purports to belong in a work entitled "Eroica"? Since its creation, commentators have attempted to reconcile this comic — even burlesque — 4th movement with the power, depth and solemnity of **Movements I & II**

The **Bass Theme** takes a crack at thematic respectability by clothing itself in a proper phrase structure and accessorizing with harmonic and melodic accompaniments

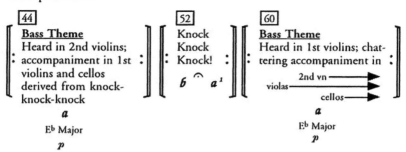

44	52	60
Bass Theme Heard in 2nd violins; accompaniment in 1st violins and cellos derived from knock-knock-knock *a* Eᵇ Major *p*	Knock Knock Knock! *b* ⌢ *a¹*	**Bass Theme** Heard in 1st violins; chattering accompaniment in 2nd vn → violas → cellos → *a* Eᵇ Major *p*

76

Master Theme
The boss is home! The "truth" is finally revealed! The **Bass Theme** is not a theme at all, but the bassline for an infinitely more memorable **Master Theme:**

winds
a
Eᵇ Major
p

84

Note: Knock-knock-knock in accompaniment

tutti   ob/vn   tutti
a¹   *b* ⌢ *a²*   *b* ⌢ *a²*
f

175

Master Theme: Variation 1
Reharmonized in minor at first, the quick modulation to major utterly obliterates the serious, self-important mood of the **Bass Theme Fugue!**

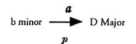

b minor → D Major
p

191

Brilliant, highly embellished passage for solo flute

b   *a²*

199

Vigorous tutti phrase features explosive knock-knock-knocks!

b¹   *a*
f

(column 2, 191 area)

Light, playful phrase in flute/oboes with chattering violin accompaniment

a¹
D Major

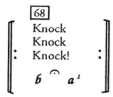

68
Knock
Knock
Knock!

𝄇 ⌢ a¹

Note: Do we really buy all this **Bass Theme** stuff? It would seem that this movement has yet to "get off the ground." Do we believe that the clownish **Bass Theme** can continue to carry this movement? Well then, what's going on here?

107
Brief interlude/ transition would seem to auger, finally, some rather more serious musical developments

modulatory ➝

p cresc. - - - - - ff

O
P
E
N

C
A
D
E
N
C
E

G7

117
<u>**Bass Theme Fugue**</u> (Fugue #1)
That clownish, whacky **Bass Theme** — the "servant in master's clothes" — refuses to accept its accompanimental place in the musical scheme; here, the **Bass Theme** initiates what seems to be, at first, a serious and substantial fugue

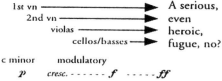

1st vn ⟶ A serious,
2nd vn ⟶ even
violas ⟶ heroic,
cellos/basses ⟶ fugue, no?

c minor   modulatory
p   cresc. - - - - - - f - - - - - ff

207
Brief interlude/ transition paves the way for another **Bass Theme** episode

modulatory ➝

ff

211
<u>**Bass Theme March**</u>
Bass Theme in low strings under a serious-sounding march in g minor; is this, finally, Napoleon? Doubtful; it's hard to take this movement seriously at this point   *f*

Antony Hopkins suggests toy soldiers at the Battle of Bakerloo: General Hooizit vs Marshal Watcys-nayme

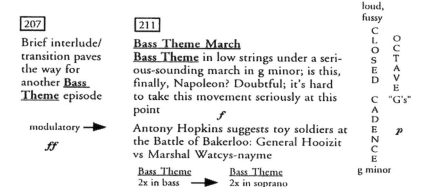

Bass Theme   Bass Theme
2x in bass ⟶   2x in soprano

loud, fussy

C
L
O
S
E
D

C
A
D
E
N
C
E

g minor

O
C
T
A
V
E

"G's"

p

258	266

Master Theme: Variation 2
Absolutely comic intrusion,
the **Master Theme** again
deflates the pretentions of the
Bass Theme with a light and
playful appearance

"dolce"

flute/1st violins

a

C Major

Master Theme / Bass Theme Fugue
(Fugue #2)
Fugue utilizes both **Master Theme**
and **Bass Theme**; it begins quietly and
mysteriously but soon builds to large,
exciting proportions

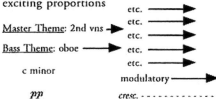

Master Theme: 2nd vns etc.
etc.
etc.
Bass Theme: oboe etc.
etc.

c minor

modulatory

pp

cresc. - - - - - - - - - - - - - - -

349

Master Theme: Variation 3 *"Poco andante (♪ = 108)"*
"Con espressione," a gorgeous, lyric and innocent version of the theme

wind choir   strings   Embellished; note   Further
a   ***a¹***   rolling clarinet triplets   embellished
E♭ Major   in accompaniment
p   winds
                                          winds/violins
                                          b   ***a¹***   ***b***   ***a¹***   <

Coda

396	404	420

Part 1: Gentle
triadic motives
**(Movement I,
Theme 1!)**
alternate with
staccato, triplet
strings

2x
E♭ Major

p

Part 2: **Master Theme**
Almost another variation,
though the theme is embellished and syncopated and,
as such, difficult to hear

violins
a   extended
A♭ Major   modulatory
p   *cresc.* - - - - - *ff*

Part 3: **Master Theme**
Hidden in syncopated
1st violins; slowly the
musical energy dissi-
pates

g minor
Pedal "G"

p < > < > > *pp*

Note: Through all the ever-building, polyphonic complexity of the fugue there is a good-natured humor here, a lightness and playfulness that betrays the academic seriousness of a fugue

ff

346

The polyphony solidifies into the same sort of fanfarish harmonies that closed the **Introduction**

OPEN

CADENCE

B♭7

381

Master Theme: Variation 4
A magnificent, regal setting; note wind/brass fanfares and triplet, violin accompaniment

low strings, clarinets,
bassoons and horns

a

393

b

a¹

E♭ Major
ff

431 *"Presto (♩ = 116)"*
Part 4: Introduction
Dramatic, downward rushing strings from the opening of the movement; now the **Intro** does indeed lead to something exciting!

g minor   modulatory ▶

ff

435
Part 5: Master Theme in horns, sounding like hunting music!

E♭ Major for
the duration

ff

447
Part 6: E♭ Major scales arpeggios, and chords, chords and more chords! A thrilling and extended E♭ major conclusion caps the symphony

ff *End of Symphony*

Lectures Thirteen–Sixteen
Symphony No. 4—Consolidation of the New Aesthetic, I-IV

Scope:

Lectures Thirteen through Sixteen examine Symphony No. 4 in the context of contemporary historical events and in its relationship to opera buffa. Symphony No. 4 is the least known and most infrequently heard of Beethoven's symphonies. We see how it represents a modest but not major return to a more classical structure. Indeed, its traditional framework is filled with iconoclastic rhythms and harmonies and characteristic motivic developments that clearly mark it as a product of Beethoven's post-"Eroica" period.

Outline

I. Background.

    A. Beethoven stopped work on what we now know as the Fifth Symphony to compose the Fourth Symphony for Count Oppersdorff. Count Oppersdorff admired Beethoven's Second Symphony and commissioned another from him.

    B. Beethoven's Symphony No. 4 represents, for practical reasons, a return to a more classically oriented symphony.

II. Symphonic chronology.

    A. The earliest sketches of Symphony No. 5 date to 1804.

    B. Symphony No. 4.

        1. In 1806 Beethoven interrupts work on the Fifth Symphony to compose the Fourth.

        2. The Fourth Symphony is premiered in March 1807.

        3. It is published as Op. 60.

    C. Symphony No. 5.

        1. Beethoven returns to it and completes it in early 1808.

        2. Symphony No. 5 is premiered on December 22, 1808.

        3. It is published as Op. 67.

    D. Symphony No. 6.

        1. This work was begun in early 1808, overlapping with the completion of Symphony No. 5.

        2. It was completed in late 1808.

        3. It was premiered on December 22, 1808.

        4. It was published as Op. 68.

E. Essentially, then, the Fourth and Fifth Symphonies are concurrent; the Fifth and Sixth are consecutive.

F. No sketches are extant of the Fourth Symphony. Despite the great surface differences between them, the Fifth and Fourth Symphonies bear many striking similarities and it has been suggested that the Fifth was itself the sketch for the Fourth Symphony.

Musical comparison: The opening moments of Symphony No. 4 are compared thematically with the opening of Symphony No. 5.

G. Structural similarities aside, the Fourth and Fifth Symphonies are worlds apart expressively, despite their concurrent creation. This fact is a warning to any who try to tie too closely Beethoven's day-to-day life with his music. Another example of two works that were written back to back, but are very different from each other, is Mozart's Symphony No. 40 in G Minor and his "Jupiter" Symphony No. 41 (musical example). This should warn us not to over-biographize a composer's life into his music.

III. Symphony No. 4 in B Flat Major, Op. 60, movement 1, sonata-allegro form: analysis with references to the WordScore Guide™ and musical examples.

A. Introduction.

    1. The mood is mysterious and magical and goes far beyond the Haydn-inspired introductions of the First and Second Symphonies.

    Musical comparison: Beethoven's introduction is compared with the opening moments of:

        a. Stravinsky's "Firebird" (1910)—a magical, enchanted forest.

        b. Von Weber's *Der Freischutz*, Wolf's Glen scene—an evil, haunted forest.

    2. The structure is in three large parts.

        a. Part 1 has a B flat minor sound, with an emphasis on G Flat. This is an unexpected key in which to start. We are again in a Beethovenian world of harmonic ambiguity.

Musical comparison: The opening of Beethoven's Fourth Symphony is compared with the opening of Mahler's First Symphony.

    b. Part 2 is in B flat minor and B minor, with the emphasis on the pitch of G flat/F sharp.

    c. Part 3 is a long harmonic progression that finally delivers the music to where it should be, the dominant of B flat major. The long mysterious and harmonically ambiguous introduction comes to a close.

B. Exposition, theme 1.

    1. Phrases a and a^1.

        a. A vivacious opening exhibits a classically oriented phrase structure and melodic devices. The main theme has two elements: a "masculine" descending arpeggio-type melody derived from the introduction to movement 1 and a "feminine" descending scale.

        Musical comparison: Beethoven's theme is compared with Mozart's "Jupiter" Symphony, movement 1, theme 1.

    2. Phrase b.

        a. This is a "trilly," opera buffa-like theme very much within the parameters of the classical tradition.

        Musical comparison: Beethoven's theme is compared with Mozart's Overture to "The Marriage of Figaro."

    3. Theme 1 in the recapitulation section to come is highly compressed and does not repeat in its entirety.

    4. Theme 1 provides all the material for the movement 1 coda, which is brilliant and brief. The coda is a Classical Era invention. The Classical Era wanted big, rhetorical endings that hammer the point home. Beethoven's codas become increasingly more massive. However, in Symphony No. 4 they are short.

C. Theme group 2.

    1. Part 1 is a graceful and sprightly phrase, a compressed version of the mysterious, descending thirds at the start of the introduction to movement I. So now we can see the relevance of the introduction to the first movement.

> **2.** Part 2 is a gentle, rustic canon between clarinet and bassoon.

D. Cadence material.

> There is nothing classical about this passage. It is full of explosive contrasts and dissonance.

E. Development section in six parts.

> The development explores the mysterious mood and distant harmonic areas of the introduction to this movement.

> **1.** Parts 1–3 represent a harmonic jungle, where the tonic key (B flat major) is lost through a slowing moving series of harmonies, and then found.

> **2.** Parts 4–6 lose the key center again and find it again! Beethoven does this by means of a harmonic device known as a German sixth. This is a slick way to move to remote keys very fast.

F. Conclusion.

> The development section is an expansion of the same ideas as in the introduction to movement 1, but taken to a much greater degree of harmonic "lostness." There are few symphonies where the resolutions of these harmonically ambiguous passages provide such a satisfying sense of arrival.

IV. Movement 2, quasi-sonata-allegro form.

A. This is one of the more interesting slow movements written by Beethoven.

B. It opens with an introduction comprised of a horn-call ostinato that gives the music a sense of rhythmic edge. An ostinato is a motive that is repeated over and over and over again. This is not a typical classical slow movement with its march-like evocation. This introduction returns in the recapitulation section in a highly elaborated version.

C. Theme 1 is a lush, almost operatic theme of great motivic and rhythmic variety.

D. Theme 2 is a sweet, operatic melody heard initially in the clarinet. It has, however, a rather strange, pointillistic accompaniment.

E. The development section has four parts:
   1. Parts 1 and 2 begin lyrically, but rapidly plunge into a despairing and tragic descent.
   2. Parts 3 and 4 see the halt of the despairing descent as the music eventually turns back toward the home key of E flat major.
   3. Early musicologists believed the development section to have been inspired by thoughts of the "immortal beloved." We now know that the "immortal beloved" episode came much later in Beethoven's life.

F. Brief digression: enharmonic pitches.

Enharmonic pitches are pitches that are spelled differently but have the same note in common, for example, D flat and C sharp. It depends on what key the music is in as to how the pitch is designated.

G. Recapitulation.
   1. Coda.
   This is a seemingly peaceful and serene conclusion to movement 2, and yet Beethoven zaps us with a fortissimo tutti (passage for the full orchestra) right before the last measure. What is the effect of the ending of this coda? It hints at something unusual to come.

V. Movement 3, minuet and trio form.

A. Beethoven calls this movement Minuet and Trio, although he goes out of his way to abuse the melodic and harmonic conventions of minuet and trio form!
   1. Beethoven's minuet pulverizes the moderate triple meter of the traditional minuet.
   2. The traditional second phrase of a minuet theme tended to be more harmonically interesting. However, Beethoven's use of unharmonized diminished arpeggios pushes this idea to extremes as it creates a strange and ambiguous melodic surface.
   3. The minuet theme is a rhythmically very innovative inversion of the masculine portion of theme 1 of movement 1.

B. Trio.

This is probably the most traditional example of the trio genre, which commonly evokes a village band.

Musical examples of other village band trios:

Haydn's Symphony No. 88 in G Major, movement 3, trio

Mozart's Symphony No. 39 in E Flat Major, movement 3, trio

Beethoven's Symphony No. 6 in F Major, movement 3

C. This minuet and trio is on a large scale. It is a double minuet and trio. The structure is: A, B, A¹, B, A².

VI. Movement 4, sonata-allegro form.

A. This movement is written in the style of an opera buffa overture.

Musical comparison: The opening of Beethoven's Fourth symphony, movement 4, is compared with the opening of Mozart's Overture to "The Marriage of Figaro."

B. Theme 1.

1. Part 1 is not so much a tune as two brief, four-note motives that can and will be endlessly manipulated (motives A and B). They have the "trilly," chattering momentum redolent of opera buffa themes. They will supply the great bulk of everything we hear in this movement.

2. Parts 2–4 express engaging, high-speed music built from the opening motives.

C. Theme 2.

1. Phrases a and a¹ are village band-type music.

2. Phrases b and c are filled with comic contrasts of all sorts, including dynamic extremes and contrasts between the whole orchestra (tutti) and instrumental sections.

D. Cadence.

The cadence marries the rhythm of theme 2, phrase a with the outline of motive b.

E. The development section is in six parts and full of good-natured energy and comic contrasts.

1. Twice in this section (parts 1–2 and parts 5–6) the music sounds as if it is building up to some momentous event and on each occasion the energy dies unexpectedly away.

2. Note the devilishly difficult bassoon solo in measure 184, a favorite test at bassoon auditions.

F. The recapitulation is full of comic contrasts and explosive energy.

G. The coda is in four parts characterized by the ebb and flow pattern of dynamic energy:

    1. Parts 1–2 are furiously chattering.

    2. Parts 3–4 slow the pace. The exhausted orchestra slows to a crawl before one final, herculean burst of energy.

VII. Conclusion.

    A. Beethoven's Fourth Symphony is brilliant and comic.

    B. Although it is built along classical lines, it is, in its details and energy, very much post-"Eroica" Beethoven. If any of Beethoven's contemporaries had written the Fourth Symphony, it would have been considered that composer's best work.

Lecture Thirteen—Transcript
Symphony No. 4—Consolidation of the New Aesthetic, I

Welcome to the symphonies of Beethoven. We are now at Lectures Thirteen through Sixteen, this being Lecture Thirteen. These four lectures will be concerned with Beethoven's Symphony No. 4 in B flat, Op. 60, and I've entitled these four lectures together "Consolidation of the New Aesthetic."

Some background, and we will allow Antony Hopkins to tell us. During the summer and autumn of 1806, Beethoven stayed as an honored guest at Prince Lichnowsky's summer castle near Tropau. There he would have been given the facilities he needed to get on with his work, a quiet room and a piano, with a writing desk. In comparison to the habitual squalor in which Beethoven usually lived, conditions must have seemed luxurious indeed. He cannot have been an easy guest. The deterioration in his hearing made him extremely antisocial, while his total preoccupation with composition caused him to behave with alarming eccentricity.

Contemporary reports tell of him wandering bareheaded around castle grounds, even when rain was pouring down. He would sing or shout raucously as he wrestled with a profusion of musical ideas that flocked into his mind. At times, he would shut himself in his room for days and nights on end, his food brought to him by servants, who looked upon him as a madman. It was at this castle that the famous incident occurred when Beethoven refused point blank to play piano for a French general, then commander of the occupying troops. Yes, the French had occupied this area after their victory at the Battle of Austerlitz in 1805. A soiree had been arranged in honor of the general, but Beethoven, upset by tactless remarks made by a French staff officer during dinner, gathered up his things, quit the castle, walking through a heavy rainstorm to the nearest town, where he stayed overnight with a friendly doctor. This nocturnal trip through the rain is evidenced by the water stains all over the manuscript copy of his Appassionata Piano Sonata Op. 57.

It seems though that one visitor to the castle got on well with Beethoven, and that was Count Oppersdorff, who had a summer residence nearby and often called on Prince Lichnowsky. On one such occasion, Oppersdorff heard a private performance of Beethoven's Second Symphony and was very much taken with it, so much so that he commissioned Beethoven to write another symphony, offering Beethoven 350 florins in return. At the time, Beethoven had already made substantial progress on the C minor symphony, the one we now know as No. 5.

Spurred by the incentive of some real money, he decided to meet the commission with this newly completed C minor symphony. But not for the first time in his life did Beethoven change his mind, possibly because his host, Prince Lichnowsky, a very valued patron, had expressed enough interest in the work already that that he rightfully felt it should be dedicated to him. It could very well be that in conversation, Count Oppersdorff expressed an interest for a symphony in the character of No. 2, and if you recall, the Second Symphony was very much of the classical style, despite the wrinkles of rhythmic energy that lead more towards Beethoven's mature style. At any rate, for whatever reasons, Beethoven interrupted work on the symphony we now call No. 5 in order to compose what we now know as No. 4 in B flat.

There are relationships between the Fourth and Fifth Symphonies, which give clear evidence that he had both in mind at the same time. For practical reasons, then financial reasons (and for a composer in enduring and constant want, nothing is more practical than money), the desires of the wealthy Count Oppersdorff, Beethoven's Fourth Symphony represents, in some ways, a modest return to a more classically modeled symphony. I'm hedging here; I'm saying possibly a modest return, because as we'll find out, despite its classical leanings, Beethoven's Fourth is Beethoven's Fourth, which means it follows Beethoven's Third, which means there's no going back to classicism.

However, I would make some points about the Fourth in terms of its classical conservatism. In terms of its dramatic progression of movements, the Fourth Symphony is very much a classically modeled work. Rather than melding the four movements together into a singular operatic and profoundly dramatic progression, the four movements of the Fourth Symphony demonstrate rather the four contrasting moods and tempos, or speeds of the typical Classical Era sonata: a fast and intellectually challenging first movement, a slow lyric respite in the second movement, a third movement dance, and an absolutely blistering and engaging fourth movement.

Unlike the Third and Fifth Symphonies, Beethoven's Fourth does not plumb great emotional angst and depths; the mood of the symphony is overwhelmingly upbeat, and at times it's downright giddy. However, and this is the big point, no one else could have written this piece but Beethoven. Its incredible unifying motific development, its audacious contrasts, its harmonic invention and rhythmic drive are pure post-"Eroica" Beethoven. According to musicologist Sir Donald Tovey, the Fourth Symphony is perhaps the work in which Beethoven first fully reveals his mastery of rhythmic and harmonic movement.

In closing these introductory remarks, I then want to make a clear chronology of the Fourth, Fifth, and Sixth Symphonies. Symphony No. 5, the earliest sketches date to 1804, a year after No. 3, after "Eroica." Symphony No. 4, he interrupts the Fifth to write the Fourth Symphony; that's in 1806. The Fourth is premiered in 1807 and it's published as Op. 60. Then in 1807, he returns to the Fifth Symphony and completes it in early 1808. It's premiered on December 22 of 1808 and is published as Op. 67. Symphony No. 6 is begun in early 1808. Even as he's finishing the Fifth, it is completed in late 1808 (this is the Sixth). It is premiered on that same cold December night, December 22 of 1808, along with the Fifth Symphony, and it is published as Op. 68. If you're going to remember your opus numbers (and there really is no better way to moll any musical snobs by knowing more opus numbers than they), 5 and 6 are easy, because they're consecutive opus numbers, Op. 67 and Op. 68, 5 and 6 respectively. The Fourth and Fifth Symphonies are essentially concurrent, written at the same time, and the Fifth and Sixth Symphonies are essentially consecutive, written one immediately after the other.

Despite being on the surface completely different works, spiritually, emotionally and compositionally, there are many subtle but important resemblances between the Fourth and Fifth Symphonies, two pieces he was working on more or less at the same time. For example, I want us to compare just the opening moments of the Fourth and Fifth Symphonies, the first movements. We're going to listen back-to-back to the opening of Symphony No. 4 and then the opening of Symphony No. 5. Yes, on the surface they would seem to have nothing in common, but we're going to look below the surface. But first, let's listen: opening moments of the Fourth Symphony back-to-back with the opening moments of the Fifth Symphony.

Musical example from Symphony No. 4 in B Flat, Op. 60, movement 1

And now, the Fifth Symphony.

Musical example from Symphony No. 5, Op. 67, movement 1

Again, granted, expressively, spiritually, emotionally the two are worlds apart. But let's just look at the pitches themselves. What's Beethoven doing? The Fourth Symphony begins with these ratcheting down intervals of what we call a third, the distance of three notes.

[Notes on piano]

G flat, E flat, F, D flat. The Fifth Symphony, if we take out all of the bluster and all the repeated notes and just look of the pitches…

[Notes on piano]

…G natural, E flat, F, B natural, it's almost the exact same opening. Granted, in the Fourth Symphony, it's quiet and mysterious, and in the Fifth Symphony, it's hammering and loud. But the point is the contours are the same. In fact, two of the four pitches are exactly the same, and the others are almost exactly the same. Clearly having written the Fifth Symphony, Beethoven was aware that there were lots of different permutations of this descending third thing, and what are some other things he might have done with it if he hadn't done what he did? and then, conveniently, he has a new symphony at hand, where he can do some of the other things he didn't do in the Fifth.

Here's an example, the likes of which are many, of very close resemblances compositionally between things that happen in the Fourth and Fifth Symphonies. I'll play you another example. We will listen to the Fourth Symphony, third movement. This is the minuet, and I want to listen for a rather bizarre series of ascending and descending arpeggios which begin in measure 4 (I'll indicate when we get to measure 4), but let's just listen from the beginning the movement and then listen sharply when I say measure 4 to these weird up and down things. Symphony 4, third movement.

Musical example from Symphony No. 4 in B Flat, Op. 60, movement 3

Measure 4.

Musical example from Symphony No. 4 in B Flat, Op. 60, movement 3

In our next two musical examples, let's just isolate one of these weird descending arpeggios, and we'll hear it twice back-to-back, so again, just listen as sharply as you can to this strange descending unit that seems very non-tuneful, very dissonant, because it is indeed outlining a dissonant harmony. Let's listen.

Musical example from Symphony No. 4 in B Flat, Op. 60, movement 3

I know that goes by quickly, but let's listen to it again, be as sharp as we can be.

Musical example from Symphony No. 4 in B Flat, Op. 60, movement 1

I would play those pitches at the piano slowly.

[Notes on piano]

It comes as quite a revelation if we again add a little rhythm to this descending idea. Same exact pitches, same exact pitches. We take…

[Notes on piano]

…and we get a very important passage from the first movement on the Fifth Symphony.

Musical example from Symphony No. 5, Op. 67, movement 1

Yes, these are indeed details but they're extremely significant details, because there are no sketches of the Fourth Symphony. There were probably very few in any case. Might I suggest that the incomplete portion of the Fifth Symphony was itself Beethoven's sketch for the Fourth Symphony? This would seem to be a very logical conclusion, considering the speed and ease with which Beethoven wrote the Fourth Symphony, and Beethoven did not usually compose with either speed or ease. The fact that the Fourth was written quickly would seem to indicate he was drawing on mountains of material from somewhere, and I would suggest those mountains of material came from the sketches of and indeed the incomplete torso of the Fifth Symphony.

There are technical similarities aside, and we could play this game endlessly, but I'm not going to. There's no denying the big differences—emotional, spiritual, expressive—between the Fourth and Fifth Symphonies. They are indeed worlds apart, and perhaps this is one reason why Beethoven's Fourth Symphony is the least known, least heard Beethoven symphony, because it is surrounded on either side by these angst-filled fists being shaken at the heavens that we call the Third Symphony and the Fifth. This is a great wrong that we shall attempt to put right by spending four lectures on the Fourth.

The syllabus to this course might look a little unwieldy. Here I'm only spending two lectures on the marvelous Seventh Symphony, for example, which is a symphony known to most music lovers and, to anyone who hasn't heard it, you'll love it when we finish with it. But it's not a hard piece, and it's a piece that's out there and we hear a lot on the radio and in the concert hall. But the Fourth we don't hear enough of, so I'm shoving it down the combined throats of anyone who's willing to listen, and I trust you all are. So that's why we're spending so much time with it. It's a symphony that wants to be heard, that needs to be heard, and deserves to be heard, and we're going to hear it.

Again, last comparison. Where the Fourth Symphony is light and brilliant, the Fifth, dark and passionate. Where the Fourth is filled with humor and magic, the Fifth, very serious German music. Where the Fourth is a celebration, the Fifth is a catharsis, from dark to light. Where the Fourth is alpha, the Fifth, omega; where the Fourth is yin, the Fifth is yang, and so forth. A good question: Is this sort of compositional paradox unusual?—two expressively opposite works composed at virtually the same time, sharing similar structural details, but emotionally worlds apart, does this kind of thing usually happen?—because it would seem very hard to do something like that, to go back and forth between these different emotional spaces.

I submit for your consideration the following two symphonies by Mozart. We're going to listen back-to-back to the opening of the fourth movement of Mozart's G Minor Symphony, and then we're going to listen to the first movement opening of the "Jupiter" Symphony. The G minor is Symphony No. 40; the "Jupiter" is Symphony No. 41. These movements, the fourth of the 40th and the first of the 41st, were written during the same week. These symphonies were written back-to-back during late July and early August of 1788. So now let's listen to a concluding movement and a beginning movement, written back-to-back, and let's hear the incredible emotional differences between the dark G minor and the brilliant and celebratory "Jupiter." First, the G minor.

Musical example from Mozart's Symphony in G Minor, movement 1

And now, the opening of the first movement of the "Jupiter" Symphony.

Musical example from Mozart's "Jupiter" Symphony, movement 1

As an aside, I would tell you that Beethoven knew these symphonies as if they were his own. What does this quick little lesson tell us about over-biographizing about a composer's day-to-day life with their particular compositions? Let the listener and the annotator beware. It's not unusual at all for a composer to go back and forth between very different works.

We are set. Movement 1, introduction, mood, mysterious, magical, a scene-setter, it creates an almost operatic, balletic image. This introduction to the beginning of Beethoven's Fourth Symphony goes way beyond the French Overture-inspired introductions typical of Haydn and typical of Beethoven's First and Second Symphonies. Just for mood, let's listen to the first part of Beethoven's introduction, measures 1–12, and as we're listening I want you to pretend that this is an overture to a ballet or the overture to an opera, and I want to conjure up in your mind's eye what kind of scene this music might be creating, what kind of mental and visual imagery might go along with this music. Introduction, Beethoven's Symphony No. 4, first movement.

Musical example from Symphony No. 4 in B Flat, Op. 60, movement 1

I trust most of you got in your mind's eye a kind of mysterious, perhaps a little ominous, scene, dark, maybe forested, and a kind of plodding sense of slow, walking motion, but very cautious motion through this rather dark landscape. If you got something like that, good for you, because there're lots of pieces that create in their overtures this sense of darkness that is then played out on stage when the curtain opens.

For example, I put on the tape for us to listen to Igor Stravinsky's ballet "Firebird." The very beginning of "Firebird" describes (and written in 1910, I might add) an enchanted forest. This music is mysterious but not quite dreadful, but it creates the same sort of mood; it has the same sort of dark, measured, plodding, and mysterious feel as Beethoven's. The only difference is, of course, Beethoven is starting a symphony, a supposedly abstract musical work, and Stravinsky is introducing a visual stage. Stravinsky, "Firebird".

Musical example from Stravinsky's "Firebird"

Just for laughs, let's listen to another such example, this time an operatic stage setting. We're going to listen to Carl Maria von Weber's "Der Freischutz", and this is the music that begins a scene called "The Wolf's Glancing". It's a dreadful and horrific scene in a magical and enchanting place, where the devil is about to come and make some magic bullets that will play no good during the course of the opera. But again, let's listen to the introductory music, creating a magic, haunted, evil forest, mysterious and dreadful, very much in the lines of what we heard in the Beethoven.

Musical example from von Weber's "Der Freischutz"

Again, the Stravinsky was written in 1910; the Carl Maria von Weber's "Der Freischutz" was written in 1820, both of them long after Beethoven penned his Fourth Symphony. I'm not playing these to say that either Stravinsky or von Weber is stealing from Beethoven. I'm simply indicating that Beethoven's introduction would seem to come from a different tradition than the French Overture-inspired introductions that had been his mainstay up to the Fourth Symphony. It seems to be much more operatic; it seems to be much more a stage-setter than simply a chance for everyone to get seated in the theater and to get ready for the music. This is an important point. The introduction of the first movement has nothing to do the classical style. It has everything to do with a very operatic-thinking Beethoven, so, as I said before, we're going to have elements of classicism and elements of mature Beethoven at the same time. The nature of the introduction is one of those elements of mature Beethoven.

Are we going to live in that introduction starting right now? The structure of the intro, it is in three large parts, parts 1, 2, and 3, and each of these parts is initiated by a pizzicato switch-on. Pizzicato means that the stringed instruments are being asked to pluck instead of bow, which would be arco; when you see a musical indication that says arco, it's not referring to the Atlantic Richfield Company. Rather, it means use your bow, as opposed to p-i-z-z, which means pluck. At the beginning of parts 1, 2, and 3 of the introduction, the strings are being asked to pluck in such a way that it sounds like we're virtually turning on a light switch.

[Notes on piano]

A very short and well-heard sound that switches on each of these sections. Part 1, measures 1–12—by the way, this pizzicato really contrasts greatly with the languid music that follows and may help to give some point to moments of this introduction which otherwise might just kind of devolve into mush. So it's a very savvy move on Beethoven's part to have something sharp going on that initiates sections, because the sections get so lugubrious and lost.

I would read from your WordScores: "Measure 1–12, part 1, quietly plucked octave B flat strings switch on a mysterious disdained B flat in the winds.

[Notes on piano]

"Quietly descending octave strings play a ladderlike series of connected descending thirds, outlining a B flat minor scale." This piece is advertised as being in B flat major, and eventually it will get there, but expectations, expectations, expectations. If you go to a movie, and the movie says something like "The 1960s: A Wild Happening," or there's some indication that the movie is about the 1960s, and then the movie begins and everyone is in period costume of, let's say, Louis XIV at the very beginning, the first thing you're going to say is, "I thought this was about the 1960s," and this will create, if not confusion, then brief annoyance. You'll check your ticket stub to see if you walked into the wrong theater (in these multiplexes, I guess that's possible). The bottom line is, you'll be taken aback because you're not getting what you expected.

Beethoven says B flat major; the first thing we get is B flat minor. We should be taken aback. This should create ambiguity, distress in various tracts. In any case, we should wonder what's going on, and let us be aware of that. These are not small issues, because in Beethoven's day a symphony concert was the equivalent of going to the motion pictures, and that's why what he says in the title and what happens first could create a tremendous amount of tension if they don't match up. Quietly descending on the strings, play this ladder-like series of thirds.

[Notes on piano]

Note this anxious and sighing crescendo and decrescendo on this.

[Notes on piano]

G flat, which then in phrase 2 at measure 6 the G flat resolves down to an F.

[Notes on piano]

This is a very important detail that people play out across the span of the movement, resolves downwards to an F. Plodding, ominous arpeggios support painful, isolated, chromatic motives.

[Notes on piano]

He's doing everything he can to dislodge us, to deny us a sense of key center. At measure 10, winds continue the plodding, ominous arpeggios outlining an F dominant chord until the pizzicato light switch that initiates part 2. Let's listen to part 1 of the introduction. I will indicate where we are as we go.

Musical example from Symphony No. 4 in B Flat, Op. 60, movement 1

G flat, phrase 2.

Musical example from Symphony No. 4 in B Flat, Op. 60, movement 1

G flat. E. F. Measure 10.

Musical example from Symphony No. 4 in B Flat, Op. 60, movement 1

What do we get out of this opening phrase? We get B flat minor, not B flat major; we get an emphasis on this G flat resolving down to an F, this semi-tone relationship—that's the distance between a black note and a white note on a piano—the closest relationship we can have in our Western tonal scheme. This relationship between G flat and F is going to be a biggie, and I'll point it out as we move through the movements. We also have this strange, wormy little idea…

[Notes on piano]

...the two pitches that surround an F, and this heavy plodding music. This introduction thus far lacks a clear harmonic presence. We're really not sure what key we're in, and it certainly lacks a clear thematic presence. We haven't heard any melody that we would embrace, press to our bosoms and call our own. Again, just for yuks, I would play you back-to-back these first five measures of part 1 of Beethoven's introduction, and then (I cannot resist) I must play you the very opening measures of Gustav Mahler's Symphony No. 1 of 1888, because Mahler begins his First Symphony clearly with the manuscript of Beethoven's Fourth on his work table. Of course, Mahler sends his music in a completely opposite direction. Mahler's opening is supposed to represent an Austrian or Czech sunrise during the summer, whereas Beethoven's continues to stay dark for a good period of time, but listen to the resemblance. It's really extraordinary. Beethoven.

Musical example from Symphony No. 4 in B Flat, Op. 60, movement 1

And now, the opening of Mahler's First, 1888.

Musical example from Mahler's First Symphony, movement 1

By the way, a word about musical borrowings, if this is even indeed a borrowing. In our litigious modern world, where any perceived rip-off is followed by a lawsuit after lawsuit, this is not a bad thing, and this happens all the time in the world of real music, or at least concert music. The difference is, even though Mahler might be starting his piece out with a consciousness and awareness of what Beethoven did, and to a degree it sounds very much the same, Mahler will develop his material in a completely different direction, because an opening theme is just that. It's not the whole piece, whereas in a popular song, the opening theme is the song, for example. But in a symphony, an opening idea is something to be developed, to be expanded, transformed and metamorphosed. And it's the direction you take it in that tells what you're good at or not good at. This is why Bach had no qualms about borrowing from Vivaldi and why Beethoven has no qualms about borrowing from Bach and why Mahler has no qualms about borrowing from Beethoven, and off and off that compositional daisy chain goes, because it's what you do with the material, not so much the material itself. That makes a difference, and Mahler goes in a completely different direction than Beethoven.

125

Back to the Beethoven. Large part 2 of this introduction, measures 13–24. Another pizzicato string attack initiates more B flats in the winds. As before, descending octave strings play that series of connected descending thirds.

[Notes on piano]

And they get hung up on that G flat, but now something happens, and I want us to really notice it, because Beethoven wants us to notice it. Instead of the G flat resolving downwards, which we've been conditioned to expect...

[Notes on piano]

...instead of that happening, he just stays on the G flat. He respells it as an F sharp; we're left incomplete. We're left without a sense of resolution.

[Notes on piano]

And now he starts doing these plodding arpeggios based on the F sharp rather than the F natural, which it resolved to last time. When you hear this I'm going to point it out; it should sound even more infuriating than it sounded up to now. We should feel more lost; we should feel more dislocated, more without a tonal center. Frankly, if we had a little more common sense and less macho, we'd stop and ask directions, but we're not going to; we're just going to get more and more harmonically lost. This time, the G flat does not resolve downwards; it harmonically becomes an F sharp. Phrase 4 proceeds as did phrase 2, but now a semi-tone higher on the F sharp. We are harmonically light years away from B flat major. We're supposed to be in Washington, D.C., at 9:00 in the evening, and right now we're still in Bangor, Maine, and it's 8:45. How are we going to get there in time? This is an important appointment. Keep dreaming. F sharp, seven arpeggios support the painful motive...

[Notes on piano]

...that same painful motive, but now centered on an F sharp rather than an F natural, and the winds continue the ominous arpeggios into measure 22. Let's listen to parts 1 and 2 of the introduction now. I told you we're going to get a lot of this symphony, and indeed we've got to get to know what it sounds like. From the beginning of the piece, parts 1 and 2 of the introduction, and I will point out where we are as we are.

Musical example from Symphony No. 4 in B Flat, Op. 60, movement 1

G flat, measure 6.

Musical example from Symphony No. 4 in B Flat, Op. 60, movement 1

G flat, natural F, measure 10.

Musical example from Symphony No. 4 in B Flat, Op. 60, movement 1

Part 2.

Musical example from Symphony No. 4 in B Flat, Op. 60, movement 1

G flat, F sharp,

Musical example from Symphony No. 4 in B Flat, Op. 60, movement 1

Measure 22.

Musical example from Symphony No. 4 in B Flat, Op. 60, movement 1

Part 3, introduction measures 25-35: First, phrase 5—that's the beginning of part 3—begins with another pizzicato attack, but this time on a B natural, not on a B flat, and slowly but steadily it starts sounding like something's going to start happening. By the way, the implied G chord, which is implied initially by this B, is a result of what we call a deceptive cadence. Indeed, that plodding music we heard at the end of part 2 has been implying this harmony.

[Notes on piano]

And by resolving on the pizzicato at the beginning of part 3, to a G and a B, it sounds like what we call a deceptive cadence...

[Notes on piano]

...which is just another way of Beethoven throwing us off the harmonic path. As soon as we think we might know where the music's going, something slimy and oozy happens to send us somewhere else. But good things are about to happen. I would continue reading: "The strings now play plodding arpeggios. With the help of the winds and some extraordinary voice reading, they outline the following harmonic progression." From the G chord.

[Notes on piano]

To a C chord.

[Notes on piano]

To an A7 chord.

[Notes on piano]

To a D minor chord.

[Notes on piano]

To a B flat chord.

[Notes on piano]

To an E7 chord.

[Notes on piano]

To an A chord.

[Notes on piano]

And then the A dissolves into octave As, which are heard five times in a row…

[Notes on piano]

…like a shot-putter weighing the shots before finally throwing it off. The point I'm trying to make, and continue to make, is that Beethoven is doing everything to keep us in the dark, but by the end of this little segment, by the end of measure 35, we feel something has got to happen, and, indeed, Beethoven's timing is as good as anyone's ever has been. He'll give us what we need in just a second. But first, let us listen to part 3, measures 25–35, to that five times repeated series of A's, which seem for all the world to finally be anticipating the road out of this morass.

Musical example from Symphony No. 4 in B Flat, Op. 60, movement 1

Measure 34.

Musical example from Symphony No. 4 in B Flat, Op. 60, movement 1

I cut us off. But indeed, we can smell the air, we can smell the surface, we can see that light right at the end of the tunnel, and we're ready to open the hatch and breathe fresh air once again, break out. Part 3 continued, measures 36–42: With great and sudden effort comes the throw. If we've been weighing the shot, here comes the throw of the shot in an intervallic move identical to the opening when we heard a B flat.

[Notes on piano]

Falling down to a G flat

[Notes on piano]

The bass now descends a third from the A...

[Notes on piano]

...to an F, and it creates what we call an F dominant chord, the five chord, the chord that anticipates final arrival...

[Notes on piano]

...in B flat, which is coming right around the bend. We have eight of these upwards throws. It literally sounds that way. Beethoven has a quintuplet—that is, a group of five notes—that just tears upwards.

[Notes on piano]

And these quintuplets absolutely shred the sense of lugubrious heaviness that's been constant since the beginning of this piece. By the way, these throws start coming faster and faster. This is what we call rhythmic telescoping, shrinking down, and in doing so creating an ever greater sense of momentum, like water being shoved into an ever sharper channel. Things move more rapidly as we end the introduction and finally get to theme 1. Let us listen to part 3 in its entirety, of the introduction and finally the breakout into the open, the brilliant theme 1 in its entirety, and what we should be thinking is: What a relief! Intro, part 3.

Musical example from Symphony No. 4 in B Flat, Op. 60, movement 1

A, repeated five times.

Musical example from Symphony No. 4 in B Flat, Op. 60, movement 1

Theme 1.

Musical example from Symphony No. 4 in B Flat, Op. 60, movement 1

That long introduction makes the arrival on the theme that much sweeter and that much more energized, and that kind of contrast between such a theatric and plodding introduction and such a brilliant first theme is very Beethovenian. On that note, let us take a break. When we come back, we will move quickly but with great purpose through this first movement.

Lecture Fourteen—Transcript
Symphony No. 4—Consolidation of the New Aesthetic, II

Welcome back to the symphonies of Beethoven. This is Lecture Fourteen. This is the second of four lectures on Beethoven's Symphony No. 4 in B. flat, Op. 60, and I've entitled these four lectures together "Consolidation of the New Aesthetic." The large game plan that we need to draw from these four lectures is the fact that the Fourth Symphony, an underheard and underperformed (and I believe underappreciated) Beethoven symphony (if that is at all possible), the Fourth Symphony is both a Classical Era work that is still Beethoven post-"Eroica"; that is, it seems to toe the line of aspects of the classical model, even while being a very modern piece in terms of its rhythmic energy, its motific development, and its odd and audacious juxtapositions of unlike musics. It's a Beethoven who's pumped himself up to prodigious proportions, trying to act like a weakling in a classical way. It's a piece informed by both the old and very much the new.

We left off, having listened to the extraordinary and very operatic introduction and then that moment of magnificent release that initiates the first theme of the sonata form first movement. Let's get right back now to theme 1 and work our way through this movement, and that will take us to the end of this lecture. I read from your WordScores and, first, just the first two phrases of theme 1, phrases A and A prime. "Theme 1: a vivacious and sun-filled theme emerges from darkness of the introduction. Theme features two main elements, a masculine descending arpeggio-type melody, which itself is drawn from the plodding arpeggios of the intro." Let me just remind you that the intro had those slow, plodding arpeggios. Beethoven takes that idea and turns it into this theme.

[Notes on piano]

And you will please excuse what might seem to be sexist terminology. These are age-old ways of describing certain kinds of melodic and harmonic events, masculine and feminine. It's easier to go with the old than to invent a new, so let's just stick with it. It is very vigorous, it is very loud, it's very martial sounding, and so we would call it a masculine phrase. It is immediately followed by a feminine phrase, featuring smoothly descending wind lines, and that feminine phrase sounds something like this.

[Notes on piano]

So jumpy and loud, smooth and quiet, a masculine and feminine phrase. We hear phrase A, then we hear three more upwards throws, and then we hear phrase A prime, loud, vigorous, played by the entire band. At measure 61, exclamatory cadence chords alternate between strings and brass and winds and brass, and then this part of the theme comes to its conclusion. Let's just listen to theme 1 from the introduction, measure 36. That means we're going to hear the eight throws that initiate the move into the light, and then phrases A and A prime of theme 1.

Musical example from Symphony No. 4 in B Flat, Op. 60, movement 1

Phrase A.

Musical example from Symphony No. 4 in B Flat, Op. 60, movement 1

A prime.

Musical example from Symphony No. 4 in B Flat, Op. 60, movement 1

61.

Musical example from Symphony No. 4 in B Flat, Op. 60, movement 1

That's the first half of theme 1. It absolutely bristles with energy. I can't help but point out that this masculine/feminine thing, this back-and-forth aspect of the theme, is within the tradition of Classical Era thematic phrase structure. For example, I would play for you the opening scene from Mozart's "Jupiter" Symphony, which we heard before, Symphony No. 41 in C major, Koechel (that is, the gentleman who catalogued Mozart's music is Koechel, so we talk about the Koechel catalog number), Koechel 551 from 1788.

Again, please listen to this Mozartian theme that has this masculine/feminine aspect also. We hear these upwards ripping throws. Only in Mozart's case, they are ruffs. A ruff is a drum flourish. {Sings.} That's a ruff, and so they're ruffs. They're not played by drums—they're played by strings—and that's okay. It's meant to evoke the military spirit of a ruff. But it has that same sense of throw, the Beethoven does, followed by a feminine phrase. Then

132

another military martial series of ruffs and stuff, and then another feminine phrase, and then lots of martial music bring the theme to its conclusion. But let's be aware of this yin and yang, this back and forth within the first theme of Mozart's "Jupiter" Symphony, which tells us that Beethoven's theme is very much within that same classical tradition.

Musical example from Mozart's "Jupiter" Symphony, movement 1

Feminine.

Musical example from Mozart's "Jupiter" Symphony, movement 1

Masculine.

Musical example from Mozart's "Jupiter" Symphony, movement 1

Feminine.

Musical example from Mozart's "Jupiter" Symphony, movement 1

Masculine.

Musical example from Mozart's "Jupiter" Symphony, movement 1

Let's read the WordScores for the remainder of theme 1 now because we've got lots more to listen to. Measure 65, phrase B, a sequential buildup features trilly semi-tone motives." This silly little idea…

[Notes on piano]

…which in itself seems like not much, but we'll talk about it in a moment, is heard over staccato bassoon playing an accompanimental version of the masculine theme 1 motive, a kind of almost flatulent sound; it's rather comic and very engaging, and then that builds up to A double prime, a last jubilant version of the masculine theme 1, heard two times, played by everybody fortissimo. Let's listen then to theme 1 in its entirety, A, A prime, B, A double prime.

Musical example from Symphony No. 4 in B Flat, Op. 60, movement 1

A prime.

Musical example from Symphony No. 4 in B Flat, Op. 60, movement 1

B.

Musical example from Symphony No. 4 in B Flat, Op. 60, movement 1

A double prime.

Musical example from Symphony No. 4 in B Flat, Op. 60, movement 1

Does that rock or what? Is this great? I get so enthused listening to this—better than caffeine, much, much better. Phrase B in some detail: This trilly tune is very familiar sounding for those who know classical opera buffa. Opera buffa refers to the comic opera tradition of the Classical Era, great works like *The Marriage of Figaro, Don Giovanni,* and *Cosi fan tutti* by Mozart, for example. This is the sort of comic music one hears in these operas, and indeed this truly phrase B occupies a kind of comic middle ground between the masculine and feminine aspects of phrase A.

[Notes on piano]

Let's just listen to phrase B from theme 1 to hear this kind of trilling comic sound one more time.

Musical example from Symphony No. 4 in B Flat, Op. 60, movement 1

What I want to play back-to-back for you, and it's very informative, is the opening of the overture to Mozart's *The Marriage of Figaro* of 1786, and then back-to-back immediately, back to phrase B of theme 2. A resemblance both in terms of the actual musical material and the spirit are absolutely unmistakable. Again, back-to-back, the Mozart overture to *The Marriage of Figaro*, followed immediately by phrase B of Beethoven's theme.

Musical example from Mozart's The Marriage of Figaro, Overture

And now, Beethoven's phrase B.

Musical example from Symphony No. 4 in B Flat, Op. 60, movement 1

Again, I'm not saying that Beethoven took from Mozart; I'm saying that they both are clearly drawing from the same tradition, and that someone listening to Beethoven's Symphony No. 4 in 1807 would recognize the tradition that this particular phrase came from, because it sounds like a lot of other music with which they're familiar, and that is the comic music of the comic opera tradition of the Classical Era. Again, here's a classical element in Beethoven's work which, as I said before, goes back and forth between being very modern and very classical.

Theme 1 in the recapitulation, I would read from your WordScores, because it is abbreviated significantly: "A dramatic and inspiring version of this theme. Note both the masculine and feminine phrases are doubled in length," so in the recap, all we get is one large phrase. Instead of AABA in the recap, all we're going to get is a phrase A. What Beethoven does, and it's kind of cute, is do his masculine thing, and then repeat his masculine thing immediately, and do the feminine thing and then repeat the feminine thing immediately, so he's kind of doubled the length of this phrase, and then does away completely with the other three phrases. Theme 1, recapitulation.

Musical example from Symphony No. 4 in B Flat, Op. 60, movement 1

That's it, so we can hear how compressed it is at that point, and that's semi-atypical. Most Classical Era composers will allow their theme to come back much as it was originally heard. Beethoven doesn't feel a need to do that; rather, he gets in and gets out.

Let us listen to the coda. I know this is like telling the punch line before the joke, hearing the end of the piece, but we will have a chance to hear the coda again nearer to the end of this lecture, but I want to play for you now because the coda essentially is based entirely on theme 1, so let's hear some more permutations of theme 1. It's short, brilliant, but short in the classical model. I would take a second to talk about codas. I think this is a good moment.

A coda is essentially a Classical Era invention. It shows the Classical Era's preoccupation with creating very firm harmonic areas. This is not to say that the Baroque Era was not interested in harmony; the baroque was a great era of harmony. But music in the Baroque Era just ends; we don't necessarily have long sections added to the end of the movement to create not just an ending but huge and convincing conclusions. The Classical Era is enamored with long rhetorical conclusions, big moments when one can rehash earlier material and then hammer home, hammer home, hammer home, once again hammer home that the piece is over. A Baroque Era piece might end with this formula, for example.

[Notes on piano]

And we would say the piece was done. A Classical Era piece might end with this formula.

[Notes on piano]

I hammed it up a little bit, but nevertheless the point is there. That was a very rhetorical ending. It wasn't just a period; it was an exclamation mark, followed by some asterisks, and then an exclamation mark with a period. This is what happens in the Classical Era more and more. There's this desire to reinforce the harmonic ending with these long, rhetorical harmonic flourishes, and these become codas, extra sections of music added on to the movement, added on, for example, after the final theme is heard, that is there simply to create a sense of conclusion.

Having said that, Beethoven goes, of course, many steps further than that. In the Third Symphony, we witnessed codas, particularly in the first movement, that go way beyond rhetorical flourish. They become second development sections, where he takes the thematic material that has already been heard and developed and develops it in new ways and, in doing so, creates a whole new level of metaphor in a piece of music that we thought we understood, and now Beethoven's saying, "One more thing, sir," and then going on a whole new tangent and inexplicably altering all that's come before. For Beethoven, these codas get more and more massive, and by the Third Symphony he is indeed indulging in coda madness.

All of this said because back here in the Fourth Symphony he's back to these very short, concise, and to-the-point codas. This would be a very classical aspect of this piece. He has no great desire to go in and redevelop material. He has no desire to create new thematic ideas or new conflicts, contrasts, and ultimately resolutions. The coda of the first movement is short and sweet and very much to the Classical Era point. And that is the reason for this whole tirade on my part.

Coda, brilliant and exciting though short, in two parts based entirely on theme 1. Measure 467, coda part 1, the masculine phrase is heard twice, outlining a B flat triad. Then the quiet feminine phrase is heard twice, punctuated by fanfarish exclamations, and then part 2, a stirring conclusion featuring five distinct musical levels: upwards throws in the first violin; feminine phrases in the viola, the cello and the basses; dramatic tremolos in various strings (that's again when the strings play back and forth very rapidly): sustained harmonies and fanfares in winds and brass; and a timpani roll. It's great; it's like everyone has a chance to do their own thing, exciting and thrilling, but short and to the point, very much on the classical model rather than the heroic model of the "Eroica." Coda, part 1.

Musical example from Symphony No. 4 in B Flat, Op. 60, movement 1

Part 2.

Musical example from Symphony No. 4 in B Flat, Op. 60, movement 1

Let us move on to theme group 2, and I'm calling it a theme group rather than just a theme, because it really has two specific themes in it, and this is a nomenclature that's used very often. Yes, Beethoven does go to his new key; yes, it is the proper key of F major, but once having gotten to F major, he gives us basically two themes, so we'll call this a theme group rather than a single theme. Theme group 2, part 1, or the first part, the first of these two themes, a graceful and sprightly themelet travels upwards through the winds. We first hear it in the bassoon.

[Notes on piano]

Then in the oboe.

[Notes on piano]

And then in the flute and so forth, ever moving higher. Note, this is really fun. We should compare this opening motive...

[Notes on piano]

We should compare that opening motive with the ominous, quietly descending linked thirds that we heard at the very beginning of the piece.

[Notes on piano]

Oh, you sly devil, Mr. Beethoven, you're just doing your usual thing, which is changing the rhythm of a previously heard melodic idea or motive, and in doing so creating something that sounds new but is not new at all. He has simply, what we say, diminuted, compressed the rhythms of the opening to get the opening of theme 2.

[Notes on piano]

Part 1, very slick, good composing, it creates unity yet variety, varied unity, universal variety. By the way, the introduction now has complete thematic relevance, because if the opening idea of the introduction now becomes theme 2, it was those plodding arpeggios that helped to produce theme 1, so, again, it's not just an introduction for shock value. It introduces basic pitch material that Beethoven then works on, manipulates, transforms, and metamorphoses but always can be traced back to an earlier source, and in our inner ears we hear that. Whether we notice them or not is immaterial.

Why do we keep revisiting certain pieces? I would suggest to you because there are links, there are sensibilities, there are continuities which may remain outside of our ability to verbalize, yet there's a sensical rhetorical whole in a well-composed piece of music, and this is how a composer can do that, by making sure that they are building on materials in such a way as to create a sense of building and progression. It's this musical storytelling at its very best, and it's something composers seek to do, but most not with the success of our friend Mr. Beethoven.

At measure 117 we have an extension of this theme. Smoothly descending phrase elongates and elaborates the feminine portion of theme 1. At measure 121, we have phrase B of our second theme; mysterious rising half-note passage is itself an inversion of the previous passage, so he's just building and building and transforming, developing as he goes. And then finally at measure 135 we have an exciting, energized cadential unit, which brings this part of theme 2 to its conclusion. Please, theme 2, part 1, based on that opening stepladderlike descent of thirds from the introduction.

Musical example from Symphony No. 4 in B Flat, Op. 60, movement 1

Measure 117.

Musical example from Symphony No. 4 in B Flat, Op. 60, movement 1

B.

Musical example from Symphony No. 4 in B Flat, Op. 60, movement 1

135.

Musical example from Symphony No. 4 in B Flat, Op. 60, movement 1

Let's listen to theme group 2, part 2, the second theme of this group. Dolce, it's labeled; dolce mean sweetly. This would seem to be Beethoven's single favorite expressive label. I don't think you can flip a Beethoven page without finding dolce on it somewhere. I suppose he means various levels of dolce, but there are times when I'd like to say, Can you be a little more specific? Do you mean very dolce? Do you mean kind of dolce? Do you mean dolce with cinnamon? How dolce do you want to be? just sweet, gentle, naïve, rustic canon—that is, like "Row, row, row your boat," with one voice following the other—between clarinet and bassoon, built on melodic material first heard in the bridge, part 3 (which we have not heard yet), itself an outgrowth of the feminine theme 1 phrase. Please listen to part 2 in two phrases, first a quiet one, and then a very loud one.

Musical example from Symphony No. 4 in B Flat, Op. 60, movement 1

A prime.

Musical example from Symphony No. 4 in B Flat, Op. 60, movement 1

That's it. That brings us to the cadence material, and let's read through that material in our WordScores, because this is weird and unbuttoned music. "Cadence material, brief, quarter note arpeggiolettes (just little arpeggios), slow and quiet the music, then we hear this shivering strong tremolo on the E half-diminished chord. It sounds like this.

[Notes on piano]

That is a very dissonant harmony, and this shivering creates a sense of Where are we?—suddenly, a series of explosive cadence chords, and then more quiet shivering E half-diminished chords, and then bang bang bang, and then again another shivering tremolo, which builds up to fortissimo, and at measure 177 a rollicking closing theme in syncopated strings which leads directly to a series of eight upwards throws, which heaves the music back to the beginning of the exposition. This is really weird and wonderful, unbelievable juxtapositions of dissonance and loudness of different kinds of music, of different kinds of harmonies and different kinds of themes. Let's just listen and enjoy the cadence material and ask ourselves if Haydn or Mozart would have written such a thing.

Musical example from Symphony No. 4 in B Flat, Op. 60, movement 1

Intro, Part 2.

Musical example from Symphony No. 4 in B Flat, Op. 60, movement 1

Cadence material.

Musical example from Symphony No. 4 in B Flat, Op. 60, movement 1

177.

Musical example from Symphony No. 4 in B Flat, Op. 60, movement 1

Eight throws.

Musical example from Symphony No. 4 in B Flat, Op. 60, movement 1

This starting and stopping, these E half-diminished harmonies, the explosive chords and syndicated closing of this cadence stuff blasts the smooth mood of theme 2 to smithereens, which is why I put on the tape the end of theme 2 and then the ensuing cadence material. It's kind of knocking our heads against the wall. We get a lot of music for our buck here. Count Oppersdorff should be pleased. There's a lot of activity going on, very unclassical in that level of contrast and that audacious series of juxtapositions.

Onward to the development section, which explores the mysterious mood and distant harmonic areas heard in the introduction. Back to the intro in terms of those weird lost harmonies, and indeed I would entitle this development section "Lost and Found: Where's the Tonic?" I would read from your WordScores: "Parts 1–3, the first leg of our developmental harmonic journey. Part 1, descending sequence based on the masculine theme 1 phrase outlines the following harmonies." These harmonies move slowly; we could follow them pretty easily and there's not a lot of problem hearing what's going on in this music. First, to an F.

[Notes on piano]

C7.

[Notes on piano]

Back to F.

[Notes on piano]

Back to a G6.

[Notes on piano]

Back to an F6/4.

[Notes on piano]

Back to C.

[Notes on piano]

And now we expect C to do this.

[Notes on piano]

But it doesn't; here's what happens.

[Notes on piano]

This weird C sharp in the bass, and again it's like "I thought I knew what this movie was about. Suddenly everyone's back with their silly costumes and their painted faces. This is about the SDS. It's not about Louis XIV." Yes, part 2, unexpected harmonic event, we are lost harmonically as this C sharp-based chord is sustained under disconnected throws that don't seem to be able to find where they're going anymore, themselves unable to find their way out of this harmonic jungle. Part 3, as quickly as we got in, suddenly we're out. The C sharp resolves up a half step to a D in a D major, and there's a sudden sense of relief. We know where we are again, the masculine phrases heard in the flute and the bassoon, and in the feminine phrase a lush new version inverted and elaborated in winds, violins, clarinet, and violins again. What I want you to notice in these first three parts of the development section is, first we're found, then we're lost, and then we're found again, wonderful manipulation of harmonic expectation drawn directly from the introduction. Development, parts 1, 2, and 3.

Musical example from Symphony No. 4 in B Flat, Op. 60, movement 1

Part 2.

Musical example from Symphony No. 4 in B Flat, Op. 60, movement 1

Part 3.

Musical example from Symphony No. 4 in B Flat, Op. 60, movement 1

We get to part 4, and with it another one of these lost and found journeys, although the next lost and found journey is infinitely more interesting and rather much longer, so let's indulge in this particular "Where's the key?" part 4, dramatic sequence hits upwards throw fortissimo versus the masculine theme 1 phrase, and we move through a number of different key areas: E flat major, G major, a G diminished chord—yes, a lengthy G diminished chord, another one of these wild dissonances that doesn't seem to go anywhere.

[Notes on piano]

And it's this G diminished chord that Beethoven sustains for so long that ultimately we get lost again. It's a netherworld, and if it doesn't resolve quickly, if it just stays there without resolving, we forget where it was supposed to resolve in the first place, and all we know is we're lost and we don't know where we are, and that brings us to part 5, sudden, unexpected arrival on an F sharp 7. This is the dominant chord of B major.

[Notes on piano]

That was the resolution of the F sharp 7 I played after the first chord and, indeed, shades of the introduction. Do we all remember F sharp 7? This was the harmony that we got in the second part of the introduction, where the G flat didn't resolve downward to the F; it just got stuck there in the middle of part 2 of the introduction. It was on an F sharp 7 chord. It was a chord that was used to make us get lost before, and it's a chord he's using now to get us lost, quite mysterious passage built on the feminine portion of theme 1, extended considerably. Beethoven notates this pianissimo as quietly as the orchestra can play.

You will notice also in there this incredible timpani part. If you ask a timpanist—and timpanists are not drummers. Don't call them drummers, and don't call them percussionists. The timpani, those four instruments, each of which is a tympanum, the timpani are a real instrument. They're tuned to individual pitches. Timpanists are marvelous and wonderful musicians. In fact, all of the percussionists are marvelous and wonderful musicians.

I'm asked very often by people who go to the symphony, any symphony, they ask, "That guy with the triangle, is he paid as much as the violinist? because he doesn't seem to do a whole lot. He just stands there with the triangle and doesn't do anything." There's a sense that these gorillas in the back that bang things against other things are somehow lesser musicians and as a result should be paid less. For being paid by the minute, of course the violinists are going to be millionaires next to these poor paupers in the back. I say any number of things. They're paid the same, number one, and what they do is in many ways much harder than what the fiddle players do. Let's face it, everyone wants to be a first violinist. You get to play the great melodies, you get to play the great tunes, you get to sit up front and look important, but it's much harder, as far as I'm concerned, to sit in the back and count for eight and a half minutes, and then at that exact moment come in and play correctly and brilliantly and not miss the beat.

I would mention something I read many years ago that had been written by George Plimpton, who you'll recall was a journalist who for years did his thing by participating in various professions. He wrote a book called *Paper Lion*; he was on the Detroit Lions football team for a while. Plimpton was being interviewed, and he was asked what the hardest thing he ever did was. Was it playing professional football? Was it doing this, was it doing that? He said, "The hardest thing I ever did was that brief gig I did with . . . it must have been the New York Philharmonic." And he said, "What did you do?" He said, "I only had to do one thing. I had to hit the bass drum once, at one moment in one piece." He said it was the scariest thing he ever did. His entire world, that entire day, his entire reason to be, focused down into one single physical act. Either it's exactly right or it's wrong. There's no netherworld about it. He said he was terrified, he was frozen, he was turned to ice. He'd rather have defensive linemen bearing down on him and preparing to bury him in the turf.

Let that be a lesson for all of us. The precision that's required from an orchestral percussionist is a kind of precision that we only usually expect from our best neurosurgeons. Yes, they're paid the same as everyone else but the timpanist is a special brand of percussionist. It's someone who's playing a melody instrument, and each of those drums could be tuned to play different pitches, and during the course of the performance the timpanist is indeed constantly changing the tuning on those drums via pedals on the bottom and retuning them, and timpani music is written out on a musical staff, just like the music of any other instrument in the orchestra. It's an excessively difficult instrument to play well, and it's a very difficult instrument to play very well.

If you ask any timpanist who's the first composer to treat you like a real musician and not a drummer, every timpanist will tell you the same thing: Beethoven. Beethoven takes the timpani out of the marching band and truly puts it into the concert hall. The timpani solos in part 5 and to a degree part 6 of this development section are extraordinary, and you'll never hear anything like it in the classical repertoire. In Beethoven's Ninth, Beethoven invests the timpani not just with important parts but solo parts, genuine solo parts. Let's be very aware of the role of the timpani in part 5. Back to where we were—this harmonically ambiguous section comes to a rest on what we call a G flat 7. It's the same as an F sharp 7 chord, a dissonant chord.

[Notes on piano]

That wants to resolve, and we will hear a solo flute rising above the strings, and then we're going to stop, because we can't talk about the resolution quite yet. First, let's just hear this particular harmonic lost, part 4 and part 5, and then we'll hear the rest of the development section. Development, parts 4 and 5.

Musical example from Symphony No. 4 in B Flat, Op. 60, movement 1

Part 5.

Musical example from Symphony No. 4 in B Flat, Op. 60, movement 1

Again, we felt one of those resolutions; we felt one of those daylight resolutions finally coming that was going to clarify all of this harmonic lostness, but we'll hear that in good time. In any case, it's time for Beethoven to take us home, and that's part 6 of the development section.

I read from your WordScores: "In a magical resolution, the solo flute leads the way from what we call a G flat 7 chord, and it resolves outwards to what we call a B flat 6/4 chord." I'd love to get into this in awesome and excruciating detail. These are the mechanics that fascinate any composer or any musician who's used to getting in and mixing up the pitches. Obviously this is not the time or place, but I've got to show you a few things. Let me do that, because the way he makes these transitions is through a harmony called a German six, and a German six is a kind of harmony that's generally called an augmented six chords. And augmented six chords are the warp drive of traditional harmony. Via an augmented six chord, you can get from Schenectady to Hawaii in three seconds flat. But you have to use them very carefully, lest you break yourself over them. What these augmented six chords do is resolve to places we might not expect to resolve to. So here we are; here is where we've been.

[Notes on piano]

There's our G flat 7, or F sharp 7; it's the same sound.

[Notes on piano]

And there's the resolution out of it, and so this G flat 7, this F sharp 7 we call a German six because it worms its way out of the key of B major and throws us right back to the key of B flat. Again, listen.

[Notes on piano]

And now we're in Hawaii; I was just in Schenectady. This is great; no travel time at all. It's a very slick and satisfying move, and the last thing I would point out, and it's so important, What makes this move happen? What allows this move to occur?

[Notes on piano]

A bass line that descends from a G flat to an F, that's what allows the harmony to pull off what it's doing. G flat F, I told you in the beginning in the introduction Beethoven getting hung up on that G flat and resolving in to F in part 1 of the introduction, but then not resolving it. In the second part of the introduction—could we call this a delayed resolution? You can call it whatever you want. The point is that relationship between G flat and F, first featured big time in the introduction, comes back to visit us right here in the development section, and it's the way we are delivered from the keys of ambiguity back home. Please, let us listen to parts 5 and 6 of the development section, and this extraordinary and marvelous resolution via a German six, via a G flat to F bass line, from part 5 to part 6, and slowly the music begins to reconstitute itself, now that it's in the right key, leading to a huge tremolo at the end of part 6 which celebrates the arrival imminent of theme 1 in the recapitulation. Part 5 and 6.

Musical example from Symphony No. 4 in B Flat, Op. 60, movement 1

Here we go.

Musical example from Symphony No. 4 in B Flat, Op. 60, movement 1

Part 6.

Musical example from Symphony No. 4 in B Flat, Op. 60, movement 1

Recap.

Musical example from Symphony No. 4 in B Flat, Op. 60, movement 1

Theme 1.

Musical example from Symphony No. 4 in B Flat, Op. 60, movement 1

What Beethoven had to do was find an even more satisfying way to get back to theme 1 than he had from the introduction to the exposition, so indeed the development does become in many ways an expansion of the same ideas that he'd been doing in the introduction, but taken to a much further degree of harmonic lostness. It's such a satisfying moment of recapitulation. I can think of few symphonies where there's such a marvelous a sense of arrival.

We have time to listen to the entire recap and the coda, and then I'll draw my brief concluding remarks, but this allows us to put together a big chunk of music that we have not otherwise heard. We will hear that abbreviated version of theme 1, a modulating bridge in three parts, and I'll point out those parts as we listen, theme 2, more or less as heard before, but now of course in the home key of B flat major, a weird schizophrenic cadence material, leading at measure 462 to seven throws, and then finally that brilliant and brief coda. Let's do it, recapitulation.

Musical example from Symphony No. 4 in B Flat, Op. 60, movement 1

Modulating bridge, part 1.

Musical example from Symphony No. 4 in B Flat, Op. 60, movement 1

Part 2.

Musical example from Symphony No. 4 in B Flat, Op. 60, movement 1

Part 3.

Musical example from Symphony No. 4 in B Flat, Op. 60, movement 1

Theme 2.

Musical example from Symphony No. 4 in B Flat, Op. 60, movement 1

Measure 391.

Musical example from Symphony No. 4 in B Flat, Op. 60, movement 1

Phrase B.

Musical example from Symphony No. 4 in B Flat, Op. 60, movement 1

Measure 406.

Musical example from Symphony No. 4 in B Flat, Op. 60, movement 1

Theme 2, part 2.

Musical example from Symphony No. 4 in B Flat, Op. 60, movement 1

Cadence material.

Musical example from Symphony No. 4 in B Flat, Op. 60, movement 1

Measure 451.

Musical example from Symphony No. 4 in B Flat, Op. 60, movement 1

Coda.

Musical example from Symphony No. 4 in B Flat, Op. 60, movement 1

Part 2.

Musical example from Symphony No. 4 in B Flat, Op. 60, movement 1

In conclusion, this is a movement of great variety and great motific unity, one that acknowledges in its themes its classical roots, even as it displays a range of contrast and rhythmic energy that are pure post-"Eroica" Beethoven. When we come back, we will have movements 2, 3,and 4 to deal with.

Lecture Fifteen—Transcript
Symphony No. 4—Consolidation of the New Aesthetic, III

Welcome back to the symphonies of Beethoven. This is Lecture Fifteen, which puts us halfway through our perusal of Beethoven's Symphony No. 4 in B. flat, Op. 60. I call the four lectures about the Fourth Symphony "Consolidation of the New Aesthetic." As a reminder of what we've been talking about apropos of the symphony in the first two lectures, it is a symphony that in many ways is based on the classical model, which in some ways is a throwback. The Third Symphony, of course, was such a modernistic piece that it would almost seem that Beethoven needs to retrench himself here in the Fourth Symphony, and often we read annotators talking about Beethoven's process of avant-garde, forward-looking modernism, followed by retrenchment.

For example, often we read that the Third Symphony as a modernist work had to be followed by an artistic retrenchment in the Fourth, then Beethoven could go on to his Fifth Symphony and do something completely new, and then a retrenchment in his Sixth, then the Seventh new, a retrenchment in the Eighth, and then of course the ultimate of modernistic works, the Ninth Symphony. It makes a very nice logical formula to say that the odd-numbered symphonies are those very new works and the even-numbered symphonies where Beethoven pulls back a little and consolidates himself. Unfortunately this model doesn't really work. In Lecture One, we talked about the proper chronology of the Fourth, Fifth, and Sixth Symphonies, and it was revealed, rightly so, that Beethoven wrote the bulk of the Fifth Symphony before he wrote the Fourth Symphony, so the Fifth cannot be an avant-garde piece following the retrenchment of the Fourth because the Fifth was actually composed in great bulk before the Fourth.

The other thing is that financial exigencies will often rule artistic desires. Beethoven's Fourth was commissioned by Count Oppersdorff who wanted a piece on the lines of Beethoven's more Classical Era Second Symphony. Certainly this affected Beethoven's composition process. I imagine if Count Oppersdorff had said, "I'm going to give you 350 florins, but I want you to write the nastiest, slyest, most rotten, gritty, ugly, forward-looking modern piece you ever could think of," I imagine Beethoven would have come up with some very nasty and wonderful ideas in his Fourth Symphony that go beyond the rather more classical outlines of this piece. So the financial exigencies were he was writing kind of to order, so there are certain aspects of the Fourth Symphony that seem to follow a classical model that Beethoven ostensibly abandoned with the Third Symphony.

But, and it's the biggest "but" we could possibly use here, this piece has all the rhythmic, motific and iconoclastic innards Beethoven could conjure up, so it's an interesting piece. I call the four lectures on the Fourth Symphony "The Consolidation of the New Aesthetic." Yes, this is the new aesthetic, clothed in the outlines of classicism but constructed with the insides of modern Beethovenian innovation.

Movement 2: a spiritual and physical tranquility, but a movement that keeps us moving. It's the most interesting slow movement, as slow movements go, so let us tackle it right away and start talking about it. Introduction, and we begin with the so-called horn call ostinato. By the way, this movement is in sonata form. Three of the four movements of the symphony are indeed sonata form, the first movement, the second movement, and the fourth movement. I read from your WordScores: "Triple meter, E flat major, exposition, and we begin with the introduction, a brief introductory ostinato, a term." Let me define it. An ostinato is when a motive is repeated over and over and over again, not a sequence where it's repeated on different pitch levels but simply when a motive is repeated over and over and over again. This is an ostinato.

[Notes on piano]

It's a little two-pitch idea that we just heard over and over again, and that happens to be the introduction to the second movement. Brief introductory ostinato in the violins has the dual affect of, one, providing a distant warning call-like intro for the approaching bel canto, theme 1, bel canto meaning beautiful voiced, beautiful melody, theme 1, and, two, providing the music with a sense of rhythmic edge and a steady pulse, which will give movement to the fluid and long noted themes.

With this almost constant ostinato present at some level or another, this movement will never have a chance to bog down in a kind of progressive lyricism. It keeps things moving and I call it the horn call ostinato, even though it's not very frequently played by the horns, because it has a certain announcement quality to it, a quality that I associate with the horns and fanfares. Let me play the introduction and fade out quickly before the theme gets going, and I want to ask this question while you're listening to this horn call ostinato. First, note that it's very distant; this is music coming to us from afar. But what I want you to think about is that as an introduction, if we didn't know that a lyric beautiful melody was following this intro, what sort of music might we be prepared for, having heard this introduction? What kind of music does this intro seem to be setting us up for? Movement 2, introduction.

Musical example from Symphony No. 4 in B Flat, Op. 60, movement 2

If I heard that separate from the piece, as we just did...

[Notes on piano]

I'm almost expecting a march or procession, or some sort of physical activity. I'm not expecting some traditional, slow movement with big, long, slithery melodic lines, and so this is an interesting chunk of music. It keeps everything going, and it does not allow this movement to fall into the quiet complacency of completely slow lyricism. Let's hear that intro again; it represents pulsing, life-giving energy that tempers the soulful lyric themes to follow.

Musical example from Symphony No. 4 in B Flat, Op. 60, movement 2

Theme 1: lush, almost operatic theme of the great motific and rhythmic variety. It's long and it's limpid, and we will thank ourselves many times for the physical activity of that horn ostinato. It's heard first in the violins in E flat major. It is followed in measure 9 by the horn call ostinato again, and returns in the entire orchestra. The introductory music is no longer in the distance but immediately before us. Indeed, it is forte, as opposed to before, when we heard it piano. It is now loud, whereas at the beginning it was quiet. And then theme 1 returns again at measure 10, serenade-like version of the theme in the winds.

Let's listen now to the entire piece from the beginning, from measures 1 to about 19, which actually brings us into the modulating bridge. I want you to notice that this horn call ostinato prepares us well to keep our bodies moving despite the limpidity of the theme. I want us to notice how the horn call ostinato acts as a punctuation between the statements of the theme, and I want you to notice how, at measure 10, when the theme is repeated, it's repeated in the wind instruments, which again creates an almost serenade-like atmosphere. It sounds like a chamber within the larger orchestra.

Musical example from Symphony No. 4 in B Flat, Op. 60, movement 2

Measure 9.

Musical example from Symphony No. 4 in B Flat, Op. 60, movement 2

Theme 1.

Musical example from Symphony No. 4 in B Flat, Op. 60, movement 2

I think we'll all agree that this is not your typical classical era slow movement. There's too much strange juxtapositioning already; it's very important that we hear everything as if this was being heard for the first time in its own context. The horn call ostinato, with its march-like gait, its reappearance halfway through the theme played forte tutte by everyone, it creates a very interesting, if not ambiguity, then dichotomy between lyricism and physicality. This is not typical of your basic Classical Era slow movement, the job of which it is to provide a lyric respite from the rigors of the first movement. This movement seems to have much too high a profile already at the very beginning to simply be written off as a slow movement, despite the fact that we all love pretty slow movements.

I did a terrible thing and I will admit to it publicly, and that is, when we studied the First and Second Symphonies, I gave the shortest possible shrift to the second movements of those two symphonies. I said in both cases that Beethoven was writing lyric movements on the models of Mozart, with all kinds of pretty embellishment and so forth, but that we did not have time to dwell on those movements given all the other music we needed to study in the First and Second Symphonies. Indeed, Beethoven's slow movements were quite traditional.

We got to the Third Symphony, and we spent a lot of time with that funeral march. It was not a traditional second slow movement; it played a very important role within the larger dramatic progression of that piece. Indeed, we get to the Fourth Symphony and Beethoven's not reverting back to the First or Second Symphonies, despite the classical look of this piece. Rather, he's writing a very interesting slow movement that doesn't act like a slow movement. Correspondingly, in the Fifth Symphony we'll talk about the fact that a second movement does not act like a traditional slow movement at all, and Beethoven will not write another slow movement until he gets in the Ninth Symphony. There's no traditional slow movement in Symphony 6, there's no slow movement in Symphony 7 or Symphony No. 8. In No. 9 there's one, but that is still decades away at this point. So slow movements are something that Beethoven broke with early too, and did different things with (and we should be aware that this is not a typical one either.)

The recapitulation of this particular theme, theme 1, begins with a horn call ostinato in the timpani, and then theme 1 at measure 65, a sweet highly elaborated version of the theme in the flute, and then the flute and clarinet. Let's just hear this recapitulatory version of this theme, Mozartian-type elaboration, although frankly by the time we get to the recap we know this is not a Mozartian-type slow movement. Recap, introduction, horn call ostinato in timpani, and then theme 1.

Musical example from Symphony No. 4 in B Flat, Op. 60, movement 2

Theme 1.

Musical example from Symphony No. 4 in B Flat, Op. 60, movement 2

Let's talk a little bit more about this theme 1. It has all the earmarks of an operatic love theme, and let me point out the yahtzees, the gimmicks, the geegaws that would seem to make this a love theme. It's the sighs, these heaving, bosom-laden sighs that we hear at measures 6, 7 and 8. From the top

[Notes on piano]

This is right out of the opera house; this is a gimmick that one creates, this sighing sound that one can see in almost every unrequited love theme in the history of opera, and Beethoven's theme would seem again to be drawing on that operatic tradition, the same kind of tradition we witnessed in the introduction of the first movement. George Grove in 1896 thought that this was indeed a love theme; he said it described Beethoven's immortal beloved, an affair that we now know took place in 1812, not to 1806, although in 1896 many people thought that the love affair had taken place much earlier than we now know it did. So much again for trying to put immediate biographical reasons for certain musics that certain composers write. It's not really a love theme, but it certainly acts like one.

Let's move on to theme 2 before we get to the development section, which is that section that really did reinforce this idea that this piece was about the immortal beloved, but, first theme 2, another sweet, operatic-type melody. Note the extremely varied accompaniment which supports this new theme. We have sustained strings, we have dyadic motives in the strings—that means little two-note ideas, almost pointillistic in their accompaniment—pizzicato strings and descending bassoons, and this theme is played by a singing clarinet in B flat major. Theme 2.

Musical example from Symphony No. 4 in B Flat, Op. 60, movement 2

Did we all notice, under this sweet and lovely clarinet, that rather disconcerting accompaniment, this very fragmented pointillistic accompaniment? It's as if Beethoven is writing slow movement themes but accompanying them in such a way as to dislodge them, as to keep them active. He could very well have put lush strings and a very thick and juicy and romantic-sounding accompaniment underneath the clarinet, and this piece would have again descended into a rather more romantic morass of mush. But, instead, it gives it a certain kind of strangeness that belies classicism and would reinforce our ideas that this is Beethoven playing with a classical style that he no longer terribly believes in but can indulge in if need be. There are all kinds of weird events that I find just disconcerting enough to smile at in this second movement.

Let's move on then to the development section, the dramatic crux of the movement and the passage most responsible for convincing George Grove and others that this movement was about Beethoven's failed love affair, that we now call the immortal beloved affair. We'll get to the immortal beloved affair at great length when we get to the Eighth Symphony, so be sure we'll talk about it, but not yet; we're not in 1812. Parts 1 and 2, I read from your WordScores: "Part 1, a brief introduction via the horn call ostinato, and then distant, gorgeous, elaborated version of theme 1 in the violins. 'She loves me.' If this love theme is the thought of her, then this is a very happy thought of her. (I'm indulging now, but you'll allow me to do that.) Then the horn call ostinato acts as a punctuation mark, forte, again, kind of disconcerting, given what we just heard, and then part 2, dramatic passage breaks the sweet hold of E flat major." Note too the sense of slow motion falling ("Help me") created by descending soprano and bass lines. We're moving through E flat minor ("She loves me not"), a helpless swooning descent into an emotional abyss. This is rather terrifying music. Let's listen to parts 1 and 2 of the development.

Musical example from Symphony No. 4 in B Flat, Op. 60, movement 2

Part 2.

Musical example from Symphony No. 4 in B Flat, Op. 60, movement 2

Emotionally, if we want to play on what George Grove wrote and other authors believed way back when, that this was associated with the immortal beloved, then we would say that thoughts of her were followed by despair, because that's what this development seems to be telling us. But, frankly, we can't really do that, so let's think of this in a more technical way.

This descent to despair wipes out E flat major, the key that began this development section, and moves the music towards the distant but now no longer unfamiliar key of F sharp major or G flat. I should explain something about F sharp and G flat. I've been saying this since we heard these keys in the introduction of the first movement. By the way, obviously that's where we heard F sharp and G flat; that was that weird key we got to in the introduction of the first movement. We revisited that key area in the development of the first movement; it's no surprise we're back there, here in the second movement.

There are things called inharmonic pitches, and I would spend one second explaining this. If we look at a piano keyboard, for example, or imagine one in our mind's eye, and imagine, let's say, a middle C, the black note immediately above that C can be called two different names. Depending on what key we're in, we either call it a C sharp—that means the half-step above C—or we could call it a D flat, the half-step below the D above the C. These are inharmonic tones; a C sharp and a D flat on the piano are the same note; it's the same sound. I'll play you a C sharp.

[Notes on piano]

Now I'll play you a D flat.

[Notes on piano]

No difference there. If you're hearing a difference, get your hearing checked right away. They are on the piano the same pitch, but it depends how we spell the key we're in, whether that's a C sharp or a D flat. For example, in the key of B, the first note in key of B is a B. The second note has to be some kind of C. What kind of C? a C sharp. The second note in the key of B cannot be a D flat; we need some kind of C. What kind of C? a C sharp. Conversely, if we're in the key of B flat minor, the first note of B flat minor is a B flat. The second note has to be some kind of C; it's a C natural. The third note has to be some kind of D. What kind of D? a D flat. So depending on what kind of key you're in, this is how you spell it, whether it's a flat or a sharp. I mention all this because the key of G flat is the same as the key of F sharp; a G flat chord is the same as an F sharp chord. It just depends how you spell it, but the sound is the same, and that is where this downward spiral of despair is taking us, back to this distant and bizarre key that we've visited at other distant and ambiguous times already in the symphony.

Parts 3 and 4 of the development: Part 3, the falling motion unexpectedly stops on a D flat; first and second violins coil lover-like around each other, describing as they do a D flat 7 harmony.

[Notes on piano]

The harmony that would resolve and will resolve to G flat.

[Notes on piano]

And Beethoven marks that passage expressivo, expressively, and then part 4, distant horn call ostinati (the plural of ostinato) alternate with falling stepwise motives from theme 1, and we first get the horn call ostinato in the bassoon, and then in the cellos and the basses. Let's listen again to part 2, that spiraling despairing descent of the development section, and then parts 3 and 4 and the recap opening.

Here's what I want you to be aware of. In part 2, I want you to be aware of this modulatory process. We're changing key, and part of the sense of modulation is the dislocation that comes with not knowing where the tonic is. Finally, when we land in part 3, notice the coiling together of the stringed instruments. Again, it would seem to reinforce this lover vision as proposed by Mr. Grove and others. The arrival finally in G flat in part 4, first in the bassoon, we hear the horn call ostinato, but then the key starts to shift again and finally the arrival in the recapitulation with theme 1, and its introduction once again. Part 2, development section.

Musical example from Symphony No. 4 in B Flat, Op. 60, movement 2

Part 3.

Musical example from Symphony No. 4 in B Flat, Op. 60, movement 2

Part 4.

Musical example from Symphony No. 4 in B Flat, Op. 60, movement 2

Recapitulation, theme 1.

Musical example from Symphony No. 4 in B Flat, Op. 60, movement 2

According to commentator Antony Hopkins, the coda has a romantic beauty that is virtually unsurpassed in the whole canon of the nine symphonies. That might be, but I also think the coda is weird, and let's talk about the coda's strangeness. I'll stop saying weird; I'll just say strange or perhaps unconventional—coda, profoundly peaceful and serene, with a questions mark. Theme 1, part 1, theme 1's opening measures gently sound in the winds. That's serene enough. Part 2, fragment of string decoration from the cadence material whispers from the horn to the strings to the winds and back to the strings again, and then, a very strange and unconventional little twist, one last powerful tutti, lest this music is too sweet and too sentimental. For one moment, we're ready for a kind of calm, pretty, and peaceful ending. Beethoven zaps us with a fortissimo (meaning very loud) tutti, meaning the entire orchestra, and then it quiets again, distant horn call ostinato in the timpani, which then builds up to a very loud fortissimo cadence, which ends the movement.

I will ask you, while listening to this coda, why this fortissimo conclusion, why this sudden outburst of noise in what would seem ostensibly to be a quiet and serene ending. And the second thing I would ask you to think about is, What is the effect of the ending of this movement? Does it create relaxation, as a slow movement should? Or does it create anticipation? It's a loaded question by the way I ask it, but nevertheless I would ask you to ask it while listening. Coda, part 1.

Musical example from Symphony No. 4 in B Flat, Op. 60, movement 2

Part 2.

Musical example from Symphony No. 4 in B Flat, Op. 60, movement 2

I think it's a good question to ask how we feel at the end of this movement. I think we feel a bit jumpy. I feel a little jumpy; I wasn't ready for that spike in my rear just now, but we got it anyway. It sets us up for the third movement and, again, a larger point is clear. This is not a conventional second movement; our minuet that follows is not going to be a conventional third movement minuet. Beethoven, while writing a piece that is based on the outlines of classicism, is certainly not indulging in the details of classicism; he's doing his own thing. By the way, we will meet a piece that does very much the same thing when we get to the Eighth Symphony, a piece again ostensibly written on the lines of classicism but so filled with Beethovenisms and modernism that it's almost hard to reconcile the two, except Beethoven just manages to fit his square classical peg into a round modern hole. But this is something Beethoven does like to do, and he does it in his Fourth and Eighth Symphonies, indulge in classical gesture while in reality writing music that's very modern.

Onwards to the third movement, which Beethoven incredibly has labeled in the " minuetto," which means minuet, a term which for Beethoven is by now completely obsolete. I read from your WordScores: "In Symphony No. 4, Beethoven was still concerned with obliterating the traditional aspects of the minuet and trio. Certainly this movement goes out of its way to abuse the melodic and harmonic conventions of minuet and trio form," and I would add to that the rhythmic conventions also.

So why is he calling this a minuet? This is a very good question. A scherzo by any other name still moves as fleet. Why minuet, Beethoven? May I suggest he's just doing it because he's got a nasty streak that's also a sly streak. He's from the other side of the Rhine, and he's basically tweaking his nose at classicism and at what he considers those wheezy Viennese pedants. Yes, this is not a minuet, but it acts like it's one, so let's jump in. Beethoven's minuet utterly pulverizes the easy triple meter of a traditional minuet. If this particular minuet had been by Haydn, the theme that Haydn would have created would have sounded something like this. Listen.

[Notes on piano]

Actually, my friend Haydn would not have created something quite so banal, but for the point of example, I have, and that is to show you a very square triple meter minuet dance. Beethoven takes this melody that I just played for you and filters it through his musical kidneys in a rather unusual way. Let me play you the opening of Beethoven's minuet, measures 1–5, and we'll hear it twice back-to-back, and then let's talk about what's going on rhythmically here, because I think we're going to have a hard time feeling any sense of three-step in this piece. But, first, the first five measures, and then the first five measures again.

Musical example from Symphony No. 4 in B Flat, Op. 60, movement 2

Again.

Musical example from Symphony No. 4 in B Flat, Op. 60, movement 2

That didn't sound like that Haydnesque example I played before, and there's all kinds of bad reasons for it. First, let me point out the obvious, and then we'll be done with it. This minuet melody is an inversion of the masculine portion of the theme 1, movement 1, melody. This minuet theme goes like this.

[Notes on piano]

And let me play you the first theme, first movement, masculine phrase.

[Notes on piano]

It's just the reverse of that idea. Again, the minuet.

[Notes on piano]

First movement, first theme.

[Notes on piano]

Just an inversion of the opening idea. And then Beethoven builds on the past. Please remember, by the way, where that first movement, first theme, came from. It came from the introduction of the first movement, so here in the third movement we still have references back to the very beginning of the piece. That's very hip; it's very Beethoven.

Back to our WordScores: "A jagged, upwards melody hurls itself skyward." What is this theme all about? Where is the beat? Where is the downbeat? There is none Beethoven starts the minuet with a hemiola. Do you all remember what a hemiola is? We talked about this at length in the Third Symphony. A hemiola is when you accent in a certain pattern that creates momentarily the impression that we've changed meter. Instead of accenting every ONE-two-three, ONE-two-three, ONE-two-three, every third beat, Beethoven is accenting every other beat, ONE-two, ONE-two, at the beginning of the minuet. A minuet is a three-step dance; by definition, it's not a minuet if it's not in three. Beethoven starts his minuet by going ONE-two, ONE-two, ONE-two-three, ONE-two-three, ONE-two, ONE-two-three. It's really odd, bizarre, and completely aminuettish. Let's listen to that again please.

Musical example from Symphony No. 4 in B Flat, Op. 60, movement 2

Is this any way to begin a minuet? Of course not, but then again Beethoven's not really worried about minuets. Measures 5–20, I read from your WordScores, "A rather bizarre series of ascending, descending quarter notes alternating between winds and strings and unsupported harmonically. Goes through 9 of the 12 different chromatic tones. Then at measure 13, jagged upwards melody returns to close off the first part of the minuet.

Let's listen then to this entire minuet, at least the first part, phrase A, measures 1–13, and we will hear it repeated. This is what I want you to notice. What is the rhythmic effect of these weird ribbons, these weird arpeggios that go up and down, especially after the hemiola-filled opening of this piece? Where's the beat? Where's the downbeat? Where's the meter? How can we possibly call this a dance? We're not; Beethoven is. How can he possibly call this a dance? That's why I said that he's flicking his thumb, if not other parts of his body, at tradition, and by using the word minuet he's bound to get a giggle, if not a reprimand, from the pedants about him. Please, let's listen to measures 1–13. He purposely does everything wrong and of course, the result is, everything is right.

Musical example from Symphony No. 4 in B Flat, Op. 60, movement 2

Between the hemiolas and these absolutely unmarked rhythms of sound going up and down, we're guaranteed not to know where we are rhythmically for the great bulk of that opening part of the minuet. Harmonic pulverization and total ambiguity: he doesn't stop with just messing with the rhythm of tradition. Let's go back to our Haydnesque version of our minuet theme. The second phase of the minuet dance has, since the Baroque Era, tended to be the more interesting phrase tonally, so let's pretend again that Haydn had written this, and we get a melody that might sound like this. From the beginning.

[Notes on piano]

The second phrase, B.

[Notes on piano]

A prime.

[Notes on piano]

That's not an unfamiliar sound, mixing maybe a little minor in, in the B section, making the B section a little more interesting. As I said, that's a tradition that comes down from the Baroque Era. But listen to what Beethoven does: Beethoven's unsupported, unharmonized diminished chords. Where the heck are we?

[Notes on piano]

Diversion or a little taste of minor is one thing, but this is ridiculous. Those harmonies have almost no harmonic bearing. It's hard to tell where the music's going, and the fact that they're unsupported, unharmonized—all we're hearing are strings of sound without chords underneath them—reinforces the sense of lostness in the beginning of this piece.

Beethoven continues this purposeful anti-minuet weirdness into the next phrases as well. I would read from your WordScores: "Phrase B and A, all kinds of phrase irregularities and unexpected harmonies; Phrase B, the jagged upwards melody continues, but in the completely unexpected key of D flat major." I wish I had time to get into the ramifications of this, but I don't, so I won't. Note the phrase extensions feature a sort of "pass the motive" from instrument to instrument, and then A Prime: vigorous tutti version of jagged upwards melody, two long series of ascending, descending quarter notes. Those weird ribbons of sound are followed by an explosive joyous conclusion based on the jagged upwards melody, and then finally a closed cadence in B flat major. Let's listen to the entire "minuet" from A repeated, then B, A prime repeated, and let us be very aware of how unbelievably unconventional this music is, rhythmically, harmonically, and as best we can in terms of these weird phrase lengths that we encounter in B.

Musical example from Symphony No. 4 in B Flat, Op. 60, movement 2

A repeated.

Musical example from Symphony No. 4 in B Flat, Op. 60, movement 2

B.

Musical example from Symphony No. 4 in B Flat, Op. 60, movement 2

A prime.

Musical example from Symphony No. 4 in B Flat, Op. 60, movement 2

Measure 74.

Musical example from Symphony No. 4 in B Flat, Op. 60, movement 2

B repeated.

Musical example from Symphony No. 4 in B Flat, Op. 60, movement 2

A prime.

Musical example from Symphony No. 4 in B Flat, Op. 60, movement 2

Which brings us to the trio, which one commentator says is "a malicious commentary on the inadequacy of musicians." We'll get into that after break in our fourth lecture, but for now let's just sample this marvelous trio. Phrase C: rustic wind band and fiddle music contrasts sharply with the jagged, jubilant conclusion of the minuet. Indeed it does sound like a wind band. Phrase D, bassoons and horns join the winds. Its strings reenter hesitantly, trying to find their pitch by trilling back and forth. It sounds really weird, and we'll talk about in a second. C prime, full winds brass band play an extended version of C over mainly trilling strings. Yes, they're happy just to find anything on the fiddles. A quiet dialogue between the winds and brass and first violin fiddler draw the trio to its close, and fragments of the jagged upwards theme from the minuet grow out of the strings. Quickly, let's listen to the trio. Phrase C.

Musical example from Symphony No. 4 in B Flat, Op. 60, movement 3

Phase D.

Musical example from Symphony No. 4 in B Flat, Op. 60, movement 3

C prime.

Musical example from Symphony No. 4 in B Flat, Op. 60, movement 3

Minuet.

Musical example from Symphony No. 4 in B Flat, Op. 60, movement 3

It's pointed out that the trio features a country band of wind players, interrupted by a bunch of self-taught violinists who can neither hit the right note nor control their bows adequately, and we're asked, How can one sensibly interpret a passage like this one...

[Notes on piano]

...where the fiddle players can't quite find the right note, and having found the highest note accent it unnecessarily? Indeed, Beethoven would seem to be poking fun at musicians, especially the country-type musicians. I would also point out that this is a double minuet.

We have a minuet trio, the minuet returns, then the trio returns, and then phrase A from the minuet acts like a coda, bringing this movement to its conclusion, again, very unconventional, very unusual. It's hard to know what aspect of minuet and trio Beethoven doesn't mess with in this particular movement. I hope Count Oppersdorff noticed some of these things, the fact that Beethoven's poking fun brilliantly at a tradition that has stood so well for so many years. It works magnificently.

When we come back from the break, I'm going to give you a treat before we get into the fourth movement, because I'm going to sample some other famous country fiddling bands trios from Classical Era minuets and trios—this is a device that's familiar—and then we'll move on to Beethoven's fourth movement of his Fourth Symphony, but the closing comments apropos of his third movement, like the second movement, very unconventional, filled with puns, jokes, and manipulations of forms that no longer serve him. On that note, let us take our break.

Lecture Sixteen—Transcript
Symphony No. 4—Consolidation of the New Aesthetic, IV

Welcome back to the symphonies of Beethoven. This is Lecture Sixteen, the fourth and last lecture on Beethoven's Symphony No. 4 in B flat, Op. 60. The group of four lectures concerning the Fourth Symphony have been entitled "Consolidation of the New Aesthetic."

We pick back up in the third movement in the trio section. Perhaps it is the trio of that weird minuet movement that is the most traditional and classically oriented portion of that particular movement, because Beethoven does something that lots of Classical Era composers did in their trios, and that was write music that kind of sounds like a village band, almost. Let's go back and listen to Beethoven's trio again. It features a group of able and less able instrumentalists. If Beethoven is indeed poking fun at any particular group of players, it is the strings in this case, perhaps some rather less educated fiddle players having trouble finding their pitches and holding on to them. I would again read from the WordScore: "Phrase C: rustic wind band and fiddle music contrast sharply with the jagged, jubilant conclusion of the minuet. Phrase D: bassoons and horns join the winds, and then strings reenter hesitantly, trying to find their pitch, but they're playing a lot of grace notes," that is, short notes.

[Notes on piano]

On the bottom side of the note they're actually supposed to get to, and one doesn't need to speculate too much to think that maybe Beethoven's trying to show that these are fiddle players that can't quite find their right pitch, and they're sliding their fingers around on the fingerboard to find their pitches. When they finally find some pitches, they're happy to trill…

[Notes on piano]

…on a B flat and A, certainly not a very involved string melody, but perhaps for our limited string musicians they're happy to have done that. Phrase C prime: full wind brass band plays an extended version of C, then a quiet dialogue between the wind, brass, and first violin fiddler draws the trio to its close. Let's listen to this, and let's keep in mind that its rustic, if not downright rude, portrayal of the fiddlers is a not atypical act for a Classical Era trio—that is, a reference to village musicians or village band. Phrase C.

Musical example from Symphony No. 4 in B Flat, Op. 60, movement 3

Phrase D.

Musical example from Symphony No. 4 in B Flat, Op. 60, movement 3

C prime.

Musical example from Symphony No. 4 in B Flat, Op. 60, movement 3

Back to the minuet.

Musical example from Symphony No. 4 in B Flat, Op. 60, movement 3

I can't resist playing you a couple of other famous trios that feature village bands from Classical Era minuets. We start with the Haydn Symphony No. 88 in G major, the third movement. It is a trio written in 1788, and, unlike the Beethoven, it describes the proper minuets and trio phrase structure, meaning C repeated, D, C prime repeated. What we will hear in this excerpt is a very bagpipe-like village band where the fiddlers get lost and start noodling in phrase D, and it isn't until the rest of the group kind of syncopates their music and forces the fiddlers to find their way back again that the group can resume in phrase C prime their music. Let's listen. It's crude and marvelously light at the same time, purposely crude. We can understand. Haydn could write the most sophisticated music in the world, but he loved evoking the crudities of the countryside. Phrase C.

Musical example from Haydn's Symphony No. 88 in G Major, movement 3

Again.

Musical example from Haydn's Symphony No. 88 in G Major, movement 3

Phrase D.

Musical example from Haydn's Symphony No. 88 in G Major, movement 3

C prime.

Musical example from Haydn's Symphony No. 88 in G Major, movement 3

Phrase D.

Musical example from Haydn's Symphony No. 88 in G Major, movement 3

C prime.

Musical example from Haydn's Symphony No. 88 in G Major, movement 3

I immediately regret using the word crude a few moments ago. This isn't crude—it's too strong a word—it's just earthy. Let's listen to another village band trio, one less earthy and a tad bit more sophisticated. These folks took at least six months' worth of lessons as opposed to the three we might have just heard. This is from Mozart's Symphony No. 39 in E flat major, the third movement trio. This is from 1788, also the same year that Haydn wrote his 88th. As I said, altogether a rather more sophisticated group to be sure, but still a lovely rustic feel and, again, Mozart's trio adheres to that traditional phrase structure of C, and then C repeated, D, C prime, and then D, C prime repeated. Mozart.

Musical example from Mozart's Symphony No. 39 in E Flat Major, movement 3

Phrase D.

Musical example from Mozart's Symphony No. 39 in E Flat Major, movement 3

C prime.

Musical example from Mozart's Symphony No. 39 in E Flat Major, movement 3

Phrase D.

Musical example from Mozart's Symphony No. 39 in E Flat Major, movement 3

C prime.

Musical example from Mozart's Symphony No. 39 in E Flat Major, movement 3

Perhaps the most famous, and I do believe the most comic, section of the village bands in the repertoire is the one that appears in Beethoven's own Symphony No. 6. It's not a trio section, but it is indeed the dance movement, and I cannot resist playing it for you now as an anticipation of where we'll be in a few more lectures. This is supposed to be a kind of characterization of the bands that Beethoven used to listen to at a bar he used to hang out in called the Three Ravens, which was just outside of Vienna. What I'd point out is that the clarinetist in this band is a very able clarinetist, but unfortunately the bassoon player—oh, the bassoon player—the bassoon player smacks of that younger brother who plays the drums and desperately wants to gig with the older siblings when they play, but of course that younger brother is just inferior and keeps bugging them. "Oh come on, let me sit in." So finally you let that youngster sit in, and they play their limited range of things that they can play. The bassoon does that; all the bassoon can play is three different notes, and it really is very funny. Let's listen: Beethoven's Symphony No. 6, third movement, village band.

Musical example from Symphony No. 6, movement 3

Enough. We'll be to Symphony No. 6 in due time, and we'll talk more about our rather limited bassoonist, desperately in need of a lesson or two, but we must turn our attentions back to the Fourth Symphony, fourth movement, which is where we are now, sonata-allegro form. This exhilarating, perpetual motion-type movement is written in the style of an opera buffa overture. Its giddy, lighthearted character is, to a great degree, the result of its unrelenting rhythmic momentum and chattering melody. Let's just listen to the opening 24 measures of this movement. That would constitute theme 1, just to get a feel for the mood, and we'll talk about the phrases in a moment, but, first, measures 1–24, theme 1, of the fourth movement, to get a feel for the comic character of this music.

Musical example from Symphony No. 4 in B Flat, Op. 60, movement 4

Let's immediately compare this fourth movement opening with the following piece of music, which is not the same piece of music, which we join in progress.

{Musical example}

If we didn't know better, we could say that was the same piece, because they sounded so much alike, both in terms of their spirit and the actual musical material we're listening to—giddy, exhilarating, expressive, fast-paced. What was that second piece? It's just the conclusion of the overture to Mozart's great comic opera, which we listened to before in its beginnings, *The Marriage of Figaro*. Again, the beginning of that self-same overture.

Musical example from Mozart's *The Marriage of Figaro*, movement 1

We had talked in an earlier lecture about the resemblance between *The Marriage of Figaro* overture and the trilly phrase B from theme 1 of the first movement of the symphony, and indeed the fourth movement seems to be within the same sort of musical tradition. Like Mozart's overture, the opening of Beethoven's fourth movement exhibits all the characteristics of a comic opera overture, the perpetual motion, lighthearted mood of the music, very fast tempo, with much rhythmic activity and excitement, and rather longish melody notes set against the fast-aced stuff. I've got no qualms about thinking about this fourth movement as a comic overture, and, indeed, Beethoven does so many really funny things during the course of this overture, during the course of this movement (there's my slip), that it would work very nicely in front of an opera, at least a very comic opera.

Theme 1, part 1, exposition. I read from your WordScores: "The theme is not so much a tune as it is two brief motives which will be endlessly manipulated to create the basic fabric of the music." Let's take a break right there and talk about these two simple, not terribly memorable motives, but two motives that Beethoven's going to derive a tremendous amount of musical material out of. Those motives are cleverly called motives A and B. Let's first listen to motive A. Motive A goes like this.

[Notes on piano]

Is that catchy? Let's hear it again.

[Notes on piano]

It might not be beautiful, but it's ours, and we must get to know it. Again.

[Notes on piano]

Followed immediately by motive B, which is so plain and banal as to be almost beneath our notice.

[Notes on piano]

Just four adjacent, ascending notes, in this case in a B flat major scale. Motive B again.

[Notes on piano]

Put them together, A and B, and we get…

[Notes on piano]

…these two simple pimple motives. These two incredibly seemingly inconsequential ideas will supply the great bulk, if not everything we hear in this movement by Beethoven's extraordinary manipulation. Let me read now: "Part 1, first violins hurriedly playing motives A and B, giving way to lower strings, which suddenly reach a tutti cadence after but two and a half measures of music. After just the briefest moment, the music stops for a very brief second." Beethoven is basically laying out his thematic material and saying to us in super high speed, "Did you get it?" Let's listen to the opening four times, and let's get it. Again, part 1 of theme 1, the first violins lay out these motives very rapidly, the low strings take them, and then suddenly, after but two and a half measures, come to a brief conclusion. Theme 1, part 1.

Musical example from Symphony No. 4 in B Flat, Op. 60, movement 4

Get it? Let's listen to it again.

Musical example from Symphony No. 4 in B Flat, Op. 60, movement 4

Wherever you are, sing along. Third time.

Musical example from Symphony No. 4 in B Flat, Op. 60, movement 4

And four is the charm for us. One more time, please.

Musical example from Symphony No. 4 in B Flat, Op. 60, movement 4

There it is. They're the chief materials of this entire movement. They happen awfully fast, but we should understand that Beethoven can do an amazing number of things with these very simple ideas. For example, that opening phrase sounds like this.

[Notes on piano]

Let's just examine how he's getting those four ideas out of the two ideas I showed you to start with. First we hear motive A.

[Notes on piano]

Then motive B.

[Notes on piano]

Then motive A.

[Notes on piano]

Then motive B, inverted, four notes down instead of four notes up.

[Notes on piano]

And so forth, and these are the games Beethoven will play. What are the different versions of motive A? He can do almost anything with this idea. For example:

[Notes on piano]

He can invert that, flip it upside down.

[Notes on piano]

He can play it backwards, what we call retrograde.

[Notes on piano]

Or he can do a retrograde inversion, a backwards upside down.

[Notes on piano]

It's not like Beethoven is sitting down with a chart of all these possibilities and saying, "I think I need a retrograde inversion, followed by an inversion, a retrograde, then I need an augmentation of the diminuted inversion." He's not thinking that way; he doesn't have to. Having established his basic thematic material, he's now conversing with it, he's now using it in many different ways, but it's the same way someone would speak; it's the same way someone would write. Having laid out a basic premise, one now uses the tools that one has created over years of study and exercise to develop those ideas. To what degree it's a conscious development or an unconscious development is immaterial. What we've got are tremendously trained instincts that have defined thematic material, and now that thematic material is being allowed to develop rhetorically.

This is always a hard thing for folks to grasp, because the act of composing music would seem, for someone who's never done it, to be virtually an alchemical thing. How could someone think of that, and to think of the instruments, and on top of all of this to think of that, and so forth? It takes years and years of study in craft, but once one has accomplished a certain degree of study in craft, then it becomes a matter of speaking musically. It's very much like all writing; it's very much like writing a poem for a poet who is well practiced. Once the ideas are laid out, it is now a matter of developing them, and to what degree it is conscious and unconscious, that is immaterial. It becomes part of a process. And so Beethoven is using his materials in as many different ways as we can possibly imagine to generate the music of this movement.

Let's talk about the rest of theme 1 now, having heard part 1 four excruciating times: Part 2, high-speed patter melody, built on motives A and B; part 3, a descending motive, finally something that sounds like melody. It might just be a scrap, it might be a wisp, but are we glad to hear it. That descending melody sounds like this.

[Notes on piano]

But of course, if we wanted to analyze that, we would say that it is an augmented inverted version of motive B. Motive B went like this.

[Notes on piano]

So let's invert it; let's make it go down.

[Notes on piano]

And now let's stretch out the distance between the pitches.

[Notes on piano]

Kind of like pulling taffy from either end, and just yanking it outwards. These analytical concepts, by the way, and augmented inversion are important up to the point that they allow us to talk about certain aspects of the music, and that's what it does. We shouldn't take them too seriously, as some in the ivy-covered halls might. But we do have to understand how Beethoven's generating his music, and this is how he's generating his music, by starting with the basic premise, two simple motives, and then seeing how many different things he can do with them. Part 4, rip-roaring patter descent in strings based on motive A, a closed cadence (that is, a big punctuation mark that sounds like a period) in B flat major. Again, let us hear all of theme 1 in its entirety, measures 1–24, parts 1–4. Part 1.

Musical example from Symphony No. 4 in B Flat, Op. 60, movement 4

Part 2.

Musical example from Symphony No. 4 in B Flat, Op. 60, movement 4

Part 3.

Musical example from Symphony No. 4 in B Flat, Op. 60, movement 4

Part 4.

Musical example from Symphony No. 4 in B Flat, Op. 60, movement 4

There's theme 1. It is vigorous; it is integrally sound, built as it is on two very simple, but two very filled with possibility, ideas—if one will excuse my grammar there.

Let's talk theme 2 now, because it offers a slight contrast with theme 1. Please remember, fast furious and upbeat fourth movements like this are not really about thematic contrast, not to the degree the first movements are. They're about rhythmic energy momentum. Theme 2, a tasty little village band-type theme momentarily stops the chattering sixteenth note motion. First, we hear it in the oboe, and then the flute. We can't help but notice the resemblance between this theme and the village band music we heard in the trio of the third movement. And then phrase A prime of theme 2, a somewhat comic contrast, the little theme is heard now in the loan strings. Let's just listen to these opening two phrases of what is a more extensive second theme. We'll deal with those other phrases in a second, but, first, our tasty little village band melody.

Musical example from Symphony No. 4 in B Flat, Op. 60, movement 4

Phrases A, B, and C of this second theme are much more extensive and rather developmental, filled with comic contrasts of all sorts. Phrase B: quiet winds playing an augmented version of A, a stretched-out version of motive A, alternate with boisterous strings playing a less augmented version of motive A. The dynamic keeps shifting: one moment we're piano (soft); the next minute we're forte (loud). Soft, loud, it's very disconcerting if we allow that to disconcert us, but we shouldn't. It should create a sense of contrast. And then phrase C: tutti explosions frame isolated motive A's in the first violins, fortissimo, then suddenly chirping, broken-up version of motive B in the first violins: quiet. Then just as suddenly, more tutti explosions framing the isolated motive A's in the first violins, fortissimo, and then chirping first violins and flute, piano, which builds up to a big, loud cadence.

This extension, incidentally, of the second theme reminds me very much of the cadence material of the first movement. You'll remember all of those incredible contrasts between these shivering tremolo half-diminished chords...

[Notes on piano]

...going from soft to loud, soft to loud, without any intervening material. The second theme acts very much the same way. Let us listen to theme 2, phrases B and C, and then immediately after that we will simply listen to theme 2 in its entirety. First theme 2, phrases B and C.

Musical example from Symphony No. 4 in B Flat, Op. 60, movement 4

Phrase C.

Musical example from Symphony No. 4 in B Flat, Op. 60, movement 4

And now let's just listen to theme 2 in its entirety.

Musical example from Symphony No. 4 in B Flat, Op. 60, movement 4

A prime.

Musical example from Symphony No. 4 in B Flat, Op. 60, movement 4

B.

Musical example from Symphony No. 4 in B Flat, Op. 60, movement 4

C.

Musical example from Symphony No. 4 in B Flat, Op. 60, movement 4

Very engaging, fun, and extremely unpredictable theme. The last element we have to look at in the exposition, before we can listen to the entire exposition, is the cadence theme, which marries perfectly the rhythm of theme 2, phrase A, and I would remind you what theme 2, phrase A, sounded like; like this.

[Notes on piano]

That's the rhythm. It marries that rhythm with motive B.

[Notes on piano]

To get.

[Notes on piano]

That's just neat composing. He uses a little of this, a little of that, and he comes up with something very new-sounding, that, again, in our inner ear sounds vaguely enough like something we heard before, that it sounds like it belongs, that it's not just a new idea out of the blue, but it seems to belong. It ties together, whether we can identify it or not, with something previously heard. cadential material, part 1: brief cadence theme bounced between high strings and lower strings, and we hear that game of musical volleyball two times. Then part 2, measure 96: fanfarish winds, brass, and first violins ring out over furiously chattering motives A and B in the other strings, a closed cadence in the key of F. The cadence material, please. Part 1.

Musical example from Symphony No. 4 in B Flat, Op. 60, movement 4

Part 2.

Musical example from Symphony No. 4 in B Flat, Op. 60, movement 4

That, of course, was the beginning of the exposition repeat. Let us listen to the exposition. This is a very eventful 1:32, at least in the performance we're going to listen to. I want you to notice that there's little transitional or bridge-type music. There's lots of thematic music and thematic permutations. Beethoven has decided, with all of this forward momentum, he's got so many possibilities with his motific ideas, no reason to waste a lot of time in the bridge. Let's just keep letting things develop as they go. So, indeed, that's what happens. Let's listen from the beginning of the movement through the cadence material.

Musical example from Symphony No. 4 in B Flat, Op. 60, movement 4

Part 2.

Musical example from Symphony No. 4 in B Flat, Op. 60, movement 4

Part 3.

Musical example from Symphony No. 4 in B Flat, Op. 60, movement 4

Part 4.

Musical example from Symphony No. 4 in B Flat, Op. 60, movement 4

Modulating bridge.

Musical example from Symphony No. 4 in B Flat, Op. 60, movement 4

Theme 2, A.

Musical example from Symphony No. 4 in B Flat, Op. 60, movement 4

A prime.

Musical example from Symphony No. 4 in B Flat, Op. 60, movement 4

B.

Musical example from Symphony No. 4 in B Flat, Op. 60, movement 4

C.

Musical example from Symphony No. 4 in B Flat, Op. 60, movement 4

Cadence material, part 1.

Musical example from Symphony No. 4 in B Flat, Op. 60, movement 4

Part 2.

Musical example from Symphony No. 4 in B Flat, Op. 60, movement 4

Neat, very exciting, very exhilarating, a lot of fun. The development, again, is full of bluster and humor, and let's look for it to parts 1 and 2. Part 1: the texture thins and quiets as sequences of motives A and B chatter upwards in the strings. Tremolo strings join in, the music gets louder and louder, and then a lovely and, again, comic moment—it's comic if we let it be. It's one thing for me to say something is witty and comic, and you can say, "That doesn't sound so witty or comic." Again, we've got to hear this music in its own terms, in its own time, and I think what follows is very cute, a big, important-sounding octave B in the whole orchestra; they all play just B's.

[Notes on piano]

It's the kind of gesture we haven't heard much of in this piece. Everything's been moving really fast and chattering, chattering, and suddenly, BOOM! and it's sustained long enough to sound as if the brakes have been put on; we've halted in front of some important moment. Big, important-sounding octave B in tutti would seem to anticipate a major event. Perhaps a B7 harmony is implied; perhaps we're going to go to the key of E major.

[Notes on piano]

But perhaps, even more strikingly and darkening, this anticipates a move to E minor.

[Notes on piano]

But, of course, Beethoven's going to have none of this kind of darkness for now. Instead, part 2, and this is what I think is cute. Big event, E major, E minor? Nah. The B natural simply goes up a half step to a C. It sounds like this strange and wonderful resolution, and now he's in, momentarily, C major.

[Notes on piano]

And now everything is quiet, chattering, and in major again, but there's no sense of resolution from this big, self-important sounding B. It's just one of these nice moments, and we've got to be aware of it when it happens. Let's listen to the development, parts 1 and 2.

Musical example from Symphony No. 4 in B Flat, Op. 60, movement 4

Part 2.

Musical example from Symphony No. 4 in B Flat, Op. 60, movement 4

Did we feel the energy of that B just completely evaporate when it steps up to a C?

[Notes on piano]

It's just such a slick move. Again, I've got to figure out ways to steal Beethoven's ideas and apply them to my own musical style, because they're lovely ideas.

Let's move on and deal with the rest of the development to the recap, and that is part 3 to the end. Part 3: varied, sparkling sequence features motive A's bounced around the strings, rising, falling three-note motives in the winds, an explosive forte pianos (that is, loud and suddenly soft) and low strings. Part 4, theme 1, motives A and B in first violins under sustained winds. It starts quietly; like part 2 of the cadence material, it gets louder and louder. Fanfarish winds, brass and low strings ring out over furiously chattering motives A and B.

Part 5, another big, serious-sounding moment would seem to be upon us. Explosive repeated chords and descending arpeggios over a syncopated (that is, an irregularly accented) F pedal note in the base, alternate with sustained chords and isolated motives A's in the middle strings. Yes, this sounds big and important, so what happens in part 6? The energy just dies away as Motive A's echo throughout the strings. Again, Beethoven just pulls the plug. big deal, not such a big deal, and then the most wonderful moment. We have to be absolutely attuned to it, measure 184.

In a devilishly difficult little solo, a comic-sounding bassoon plays Theme 1 in anticipation of the recap. Is the bassoonist lost? Is the bassoon just over-enthusiastic? Is the bassoonist nuts? It's very hard to play, and it's very funny. What's the bassoonist trying to do? I would tell you that every bassoonist has to play this excerpt in their juries and in their auditions. It's just one of those bassoon excerpts that will follow every bassoonist around until the day they die. Low strings continue with motives A and B, and we slip right into the recap. Let us listen to part 3 through the recap opening, and be especially attuned for the bassoon solo that occurs in the second half of part 6. Part 3.

Musical example from Symphony No. 4 in B Flat, Op. 60, movement 4

Part 4.

Musical example from Symphony No. 4 in B Flat, Op. 60, movement 4

Part 5.

Musical example from Symphony No. 4 in B Flat, Op. 60, movement 4

Part 6.

Musical example from Symphony No. 4 in B Flat, Op. 60, movement 4

Recapitulation.

Musical example from Symphony No. 4 in B Flat, Op. 60, movement 4

It's a great moment, and I love that bassoon solo, and it's one of those tests by fire. Say the Fourth Symphony to a bassoonist, and they will flush and their skin will grow moist and warm in anticipation—recapitulation, a rip-roaring and marvelous chunk of music, as was the expo, filled with comic contrast and great rhythmic energy.

I would take one second to talk about that bassoon solo, because I'm going to have a couple of seconds. It's a very interesting question that I'm asked between lectures, and the question is, "How do composers think?" First of all, you're assuming that composers think by being asked that question, but, yes, they think. But do they think instrumentally, or do they compose their music first and then arrange it, orchestrate it for the instruments? Of course, there's no single answer to that question. It very much depends on the composer; it depends on the era; it depends on whether they are an orchestral composer or not.

For example, Gustav Mahler, the great Czech-born but Viennese-bred symphonist of the turn of the 20th century, sketched everything out for two pianos for his First, Second, Third, and Fourth symphonies. He wrote it as if it was a two-piano piece, and then orchestrated. He did that during the summer and orchestrated during the fall and winter. But starting with his Fifth Symphony, Mahler said, "Enough of that. I'm hearing orchestrally," and starting with this Fifth Symphony Mahler simply composed right onto the sheets of orchestral paper. This is the flutes, this is the clarinets, this is the bassoons and so forth. Other composers, like Stravinsky, for example, will write out very carefully as if the piece was for one or two pianos, but indicate with different colored ink what instruments will play what, and then will go back and do a full score. Still other composers always compose for full score, and other composers just compose for piano and then arrange it.

Certain aspects of any piece like this Fourth Symphony clearly are based on traditional orchestration techniques. For example, when we hear a theme—let's say the first theme in the first movement—there's a way of orchestrating a theme that would be accepted by Beethoven's era, and that would be to use basically the first violins and have the other instruments support the first violins. So Beethoven doesn't have to indicate anything special about that orchestration; he's just going to use a stock orchestrational technique in that first theme. But then there's that bassoon solo we just heard that could not have been conceived on any other instrument. That could not have been conceived unless Beethoven was, in his ear while he was composing saying, "This is going to be great; I'm going to have a very comic and funny—because the bassoon tends to be comic and funny—a very wonderful comic bassoon solo in anticipation of the first theme in the recap, and it's just going to be one of these great moments for the bassoonist. He has to have conceived that for the bassoon.

In some cases, even within a single piece of music, the composer is thinking of things generically and conceiving other things specific to the instruments that will play them. So it's not an easy question to answer, and one would like to think one can look at sketches and determine through sketches, but often they are not adequate because a composer will just write an idea down, already having decided in their mind which instrument will play that, but they don't make good on that decision until they actually write the score.

Onward to the coda, please. The orchestra finally runs out of steam. Coda, parts 1 and 2: again, contrast and furiously chattering melodies. Part 1, much like part 1 of the development, suddenly quiet upward sequence of motives A and B; then we have syncopated exclamatory chords and quiet motive A's in the violins. Theme 1: a whispering version of the theme is heard in the first violins, clarinet, and bassoon. Part 2: huge cadential unit, explosive chords, and furiously chattering strings arrive on a very important-sounding F dominant 7 chord.

[Notes on piano]}

But we know what has happened to important-sounding moments in this movement up to this point. Please, Coda, parts 1 and 2.

Musical example from Symphony No. 4 in B Flat, Op. 60, movement 4

Part 2.

Musical example from Symphony No. 4 in B Flat, Op. 60, movement 4

A pause, a long, sustained idea, where is this going? Let's look. Part 3, the descending motive (that is, part 3 of theme 1) appears in strings and winds over motives A and B. They are accompanied by thoroughly overworked low strings. Part 4, quiet winds in dialogue with low strings playing an unaltered version of motive A. The strings manage one last burst of energy, entering with motives A and B against augmented winds. We hear this big tri-tone, this big dissonance.

[Notes on piano]

Another pause, and then a big F.

[Notes on piano]

Another pause, and that's it. They're out of steam. That's the best they can do. What more do we want from these poor players? Tired, worn-out first violins play an augmented version of theme 1 quietly, then they stop, and there's a pause. Then an exhausted bassoon—and the bassoonist should be exhausted—plays a single motive B, and then stops and pauses, and then equally tired violins and violas answer the bassoon. "You think you're tired? I'm going to tell you how tired we are," and another pause. And just when we think that the symphony has died on the vine, an explosive finale, one last Herculean burst of energy brings the movement and the symphony to a lively conclusion. Very cute, very funny, very effective. Coda, part 3, to the end.

Musical example from Symphony No. 4 in B Flat, Op. 60, movement 4

Part 4.

Musical example from Symphony No. 4 in B Flat, Op. 60, movement 4

Tri-tone. F's.

Musical example from Symphony No. 4 in B Flat, Op. 60, movement 4

Conclusions: the Fourth Symphony of Beethoven is a brilliant, comic, effervescent symphony. It is built along classical lines but pure post-"Eroica" Beethoven in all of its important details. If any of Beethoven's contemporaries had written this symphony, it would be considered that composers masterwork, and that composer would be remembered forever for the symphony, and the symphony would be played lots as an example of that composer's great work. As it is, for Beethoven it is a work in search of an audience. It's the least known and least appreciated of the nine. So let us all spread the gospel of Beethoven's Fourth Symphony, a symphony, as we knew already but now know for sure, that is wholly worthy of our best attention.

This page left intentionally blank.

MOVEMENT I *Sonata-Allegro form* duple meter (4/4)

Introduction

Invokes a strange and mysterious musical world, one far away from B♭ Major

"Adagio (♩ = 66)"

2

P
A
R
T

1

Phrase 1: Quietly plucked octave B♭ strings "switch on" a mysterious, sustained B♭ in the winds

pp

Quietly descending octave strings play a "ladder-like" series of connected, descending 3rds, outlining a b♭ minor collection, 1–6:

Note anxious, sighing < > on octave "G♭"

↓

13

P
A
R
T

2

Phrase 3: *forte* pizzicato strings again initiate octave B♭s in the winds

f > *pp*

As before, descending octave strings play a series of connected, descending 3rds, outlining a b♭ minor collection

pp

Strings come to rest on octave "G♭"

25

P
A
R
T

3

Phrase 5: *forte* pizzicato strings ("G–B") again initiate sustained octaves in winds, this time a B♮

Note: the implied G chord initially acts as a deceptive (VI of b) resolution to the previous F♯⁷ chord

f

Strings now play plodding arpeggios; with the help of the winds and some extraordinary voice-leading, they outline the following harmonic progression:

G⁷ C A⁷ d B♭ E⁷ A⁷ d A⁷

Where is all of this heading?

Op. 60 (1806)

6

Phrase 2: "G♭" (6̂ of b♭ minor) resolves downwards to "F"; plodding ominous arpeggios support painful, isolated chromatic motives (G♭ ➤ E ➤ F)

  bassoon + cellos and basses

  pp

10

Winds continue the plodding, ominous arpeggios (outlining F7) until . . .

  pp

18

Phrase 4: This time, the "G♭" does <u>not</u> resolve downwards; it enharmonically becomes an F#. **Phrase 4** procedes as did **Phrase 2**, but now a <u>semitone higher</u>! We are harmonic light years away from B♭ Major! Arpeggios support painful motive (G ➤ E# ➤ F) in:

  bassoon + cellos and basses

  pp

22

Winds continue the ominous arpeggios (outlining F#7, V of b minor) until . . .

  pp

34

A7 dissolves into octave "A"s, themselves repeated <u>5 times</u> "like a shot-putter weighing his shot before throwing it" (A. Hopkins)

  pp ◁

36

With great and sudden effort comes the "throw":

<u>Note!</u>: in an intervallic move identical to octave "B♭–G♭" (ms 1–2), the bass descends a major 3rd from octave "A" to "F", creating an F7 chord!!! (V of B♭)

<u>Eight</u> subsequent upwards "throws" heave the music headlong into the Allegro . . .   *ff*

185

Exposition
"Allegro vivace ($\bullet$ = 80)"

43

Theme 1

A vivacious, sun-filled theme emerges from the darkness of the **Intro**   53

| Theme features <u>two</u> main elements:
1) "masculine" descending arpeggio-
type melody (drawn from plodding
arpeggios of **Introduction**)
2) "feminine" phrase features smoothly
descending wind line | Three
more
upwards
"throws" | tutti
*a*¹
ff |

a

B♭ Major

p

89

Modulating Bridge: Grows directly out of "*a*²"

95   103

| Part 1:
Rising sequence
based on the
"masculine"
Theme 1 motive | Part 2:
Restless,
syncopated
chords | Part 3:
Smooth, "feminine"
melody in viola/cello
segues into . . . |

ff   *ff*

winds ➡ tutti

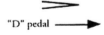

"D" pedal ⟶

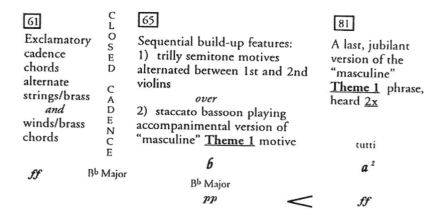

61		65	81
Exclamatory cadence chords alternate strings/brass *and* winds/brass chords	C L O S E D C A D E N C E	Sequential build-up features: 1) trilly semitone motives alternated between 1st and 2nd violins *over* 2) staccato bassoon playing accompanimental version of "masculine" **Theme 1** motive	A last, jubilant version of the "masculine" **Theme 1** phrase, heard 2x

ff   Bb Major

6

Bb Major

pp   <   *ff*

tutti

a²

107

Theme Group 2

Part 1: A graceful and sprightly themelette travels upwards through the winds:

a

F Major

p

(Note: Compare the opening 8th-note motive to the ominous, quietly descending linked 3rds of the **Introduction** ms 2–3:

187

117	121	135
Extension: smoothly descending phrase elongates and elaborates the "feminine" portion of **Theme 1**	Mysteriously rising 1/2-note passage is itself a free inversion of the previous passage	Exciting, energized cadential unit brings this part of **Theme 2** to a close
p	b p $<$	f

149	157				
	Cadence Material				
Vigorous tutti version of the canon	Brief 1/4-note arpeggios slow and quiet the music	Shivering string tremolo E$^{\sharp 7}$ (VII$^{\sharp 7}$ of F)	E X P L O S I V E — C A D E N C E · C H O R D S	Shivering string tremolo E$^{\sharp 7}$	E X P L O S I V E — C A D E N C E · C H O R D S
a^1					
ff	p	pp		pp	

Development

187

Part 1: Descending sequence based on the "masculine" **Theme 1** phrase, outlines the following, slowly moving harmonies:

F - C^7 - F - g^6 - F$^{\sharp}$ - C - A^6!
4ms 4ms 2ms 2ms   2ms

203

Part 2: <u>Unexpected</u> harmonic event! We are "lost" harmonically, as this C$^{\sharp}$-based chord is sustained under disconnected "throws," themselves unable to find their way out of this harmonic jungle!

Theme Group 2

Part 2: "*dolce*," gentle, rustic canon between clarinet and bassoon; built on melodic material 1st heard in the **Modulating Bridge, Part 3**, itself an outgrowth of the "feminine" **Theme 1** phrase:

a
F Major
p

<table>
<tr><td>167</td><td>177</td><td>185</td></tr>
<tr>
<td>Shivering
string
tremolos</td>
<td>Rollicking
closing theme in
syncopated
strings!</td>
<td>1.
Series of <u>8</u> upward
throws heaves the
music back into the
Exposition!</td>
</tr>
</table>

pp < *ff*

217
Part 3: We're out!
Theme 1
"masculine" phrase
in:

flute ➤ bassoon
    D Major
    p

225
"Feminine" phrase;
lush new version,
inverted and
elaborated in:

winds ➤ violins ➤ clarinet ➤ violins

(Note: "masculine"
phrase in accomp.)

modulation ————————————➤

| 241 |

Part 4: Dramatic sequence pits upwards "throw" ($f\!f$)

vs

"masculine" **Theme 1** phrase (p)

<u>3x total</u>

1st	2nd	3rd	lengthy
E♭ Major	G Major	G°7	extension of G°7 . . .

f	p	f	p	$f\!f$	f

>

| 281 |

Part 5: Sudden, unexpected arrival on F#7 (V of B) (shades of the **Introduction!**) Quiet, mysterious passage built on the "feminine" portion of **Theme 1**, extended considerably

ppp pp

| 305 |

Part 6: <u>Retransition</u>
In a magical resolution, the solo flute leads the way as the <u>G♭</u> triad resolves outwards to a B♭$^6_4$ (I$^6_4$)

| 312 |

Now in the "right" key, rising motives begin to accumulate over a rolling timpani, the rising motives grow in power and volume until . . .

pp *cresc.* . . . . . .

Recapitulation

| 337 |

<u>Theme 1</u>
Abbreviated, initially dramatic and inspiring version of this originally quiet theme

<u>Note</u>: both "masculine" and "feminine" phrases doubled in length

"masculine"		"feminine"	
tutti	oboe	strings/flute	winds
B♭ Major			

$f\!f$	p	p	p

<

| 351 |

Modulating Bridge
Grows directly out of <u>Theme 1</u>:

Part 1:
Rising sequence based on "masculine" **Theme 1** phrase

| 369 |
Part 2:
Restless, syncopated chords grow from:

winds ➔ tutti

| 377 |
Part 3:
Smooth, "feminine" melody in viola and cello segues into . . .

$f\!f$ p

(Note syncopations)

This harmonically ambiguous section comes to rest on a G♭
Major (enharmonically F♯ Major) triad; a solo flute rises
above the strings and . . .

333

Huge string
tremolo

ff

381

Theme Group 2

Part 1: Graceful and
sprightly themelette
travels upwards
through the winds

391

Extension:
smoothly
descending
flutes and
violins

395

Mysterious,
rising 1/2-note
passage is itself
a free inversion
of previous
flute/violin
passage

406

Excited,
energized
cadential
unit

a

B♭ Major

p

p

b

pp

f

191

Theme Group 2

Part 2: "*dolce*" canon,
heard 2x, between:

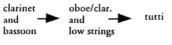

1st canon

p

2nd canon

f

431

Cadence Material

Brief 1/4-
note
arpeggios
quiet and
slow the
action

p

Shivering
string tremolo
on an A$^{\sharp}$7
(VII$^{\sharp}$7 of Bb)

pp

E
X
P
L
O
S
I
V
E

C
A
D
E
N
C
E

C
H
O
R
D
S

ff

Coda

467

Part 1: <u>Theme 1</u>
"masculine" phrase
heard <u>twice</u>; outlines
Bb Major triad

ff

475

Quiet "feminine" phrase
heard <u>twice</u>, punctuated by
fanfarish tutti exclamations

p *f*   *p* *f*

			441		451	462

Shivering string tremolo

(A♯7)

pp

E X P L O S I V E **C A D E N C E C H O R D S**

ff

Shivering string tremolo

pp <

Rollicking closing theme in syncopated strings

ff

⌒
F7

ff

Seven upward "throws" lead directly into . . .

F7

483

Part 2: Stirring conclusion features <u>five</u> distinct musical levels:
1) Upward "throws" in 1st violins
2) "Feminine" phrases in viola/cello/basses
3) Dramatic tremolos in various strings
4) Sustained harmonies/fanfares in winds and brass
5) Timpani roll

MOVEMENT II *quasi Sonata-Allegro form*

"Adagio (♩ = 84)"   (triple meter, E♭ Major)

Exposition

Introduction:  Horn-call ostinato

Brief introductory ostinato in the violins has the dual effect of:
1) Providing a distant, horn-call-like introduction for the approaching
bel canto-like **Theme 1**
2) Providing the music with a sense of rhythmic edge and steady
pulse which will give movement to the fluid and long-noted themes

E♭ Major

9

Horn-call ostinato

returns in tutti; the music is
no longer " in the distance"
but immediately before us

f

10

Theme 1
Serenade-like version of the
theme in the winds

E♭ Major

p

26

Theme 2
Another sweet, operatic-like melody; note extremely
varied accompaniment which supports this new theme:
– sustained strings   – pizzicato strings
– diadic motives in strings   – descending bassoons

clarinet
p
B♭ Major

f

33

tutti
cadence

2

Theme 1

Lush, almost operatic theme of great motivic and rhythmic variety:

violins
E♭ Major
p

17

Modulating Bridge

Sequence in 2 parts:

Dramatic string
arpeggios and
brass/wind fanfares
f

Sweet, fluid
melody in winds
and 1st violins
p

3x total

23

Extension of 3rd
sequential phrase
sustains the V7/V
(F7) harmony,
allowing a modulation
to V (B♭ Major)

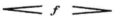 *f*

34

Cadence Material

Part 1: Brief Cadence Theme:

bassoons ➔ winds
B♭ Major
p

Part 2: Tutti build-up based on
the rhythm of the

Horn-call ostinato

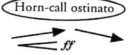 *ff*

Note: Horn-call ostinato

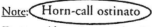

Decorated by strings, underpins this part

Note: Music modulates back toward
the original tonic E♭ Major ➔

Development (brief)

41

Part I:
Brief introduction

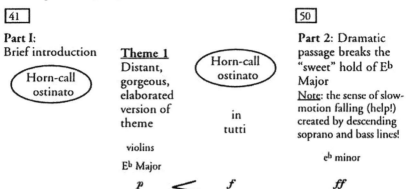

Horn-call ostinato

Theme 1
Distant, gorgeous, elaborated version of theme

violins

E♭ Major

p < *f*

Horn-call ostinato

in tutti

50

Part 2: Dramatic passage breaks the "sweet" hold of E♭ Major

Note: the sense of slow-motion falling (help!) created by descending soprano and bass lines!

e♭ minor

ff

Recapitulation

64

Introduction

Horn-call ostinato

in timpani

65

Theme 1
Sweet, highly elaborated version in the:

flute ➡ flute/clarinet

E♭ Major

p <

89

Cadence Material
Part 1: Brief cadence theme in:

horns ➡ winds ➡

E♭ Major

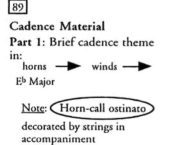

Note: Horn-call ostinato

decorated by strings in accompaniment

p

93

Part 2: Fragments of the string decoration (**Part 1**) descend, "*perdendo*" ("dying away"):

1st violins

violas

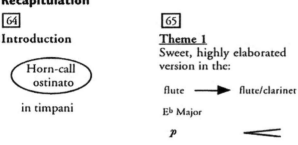

cellos

54

Part 3: The falling motion unexpectedly stops on a "Dᵇ"; 1st and 2nd violins coil, lover-like, around each other, describing as they do a Dᵇ7 harmony (V of Gᵇ, III of eᵇ minor)

"*espressivo*"

p

 59

Part 4: Sequence:

Distant (Horn-call ostinatos) alternate with falling stepwise motive from **Theme 1** opening:

appears in:

bassoon ➔ cello/basses
Gᵇ Major   cᵇ minor

72

Modulating Bridge
Sequence in 2 parts:

Dramatic string arpeggios and brass/wind fanfares
f

Sweet, fluid melody in winds and 1st violins
p

3x total

Extension of 3rd sequential phrase sustains Bᵇ7 (V7 of Eᵇ) harmony
$< f >$

??

Theme 2
Sweet, operatic melody

clarinet
EᵇMajor
p $< f$

tutti cadence

Coda Profoundly peaceful and serene conclusion

96

Part 1:
Theme 1
opening measures gently sound in winds
Eᵇ Major
pp

98

Part 2:
Fragment of string decoration (from **Cadence Material**) whisper from:

strings ➔ winds
horns   strings
$<$

One last powerful tutti, lest this music gets too sweet and sentimental
ff

102

Distant

(Horn-call ostinato)

in timpani
pp $<$ ff

C
A
D
E
N
C
E

MOVEMENT III   *Minuet & Trio* (sure! . . . *Scherzo!*)

In his *Symphony No. 4*, Beethoven was still concerned with obliterating the traditional aspects of a Minuet & Trio; certainly this movement goes out of its way to abuse the melodic and harmonic conventions of Minuet & Trio form!

"Allegro vivace (♩. = 100)"   triple meter (3/4)

Minuet

A jagged, upwards melody (note <u>rests</u>!) hurls itself upwards: ⟶

6

The jagged, upwards melody continues, but in the completely unexpected key of D♭ Major!

Note: Phrase extensions feature a sort of "pass-the-motive" from instrument to instrument

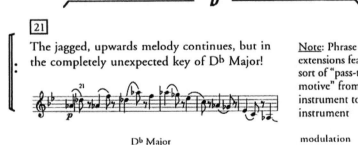

D♭ Major

modulation ⟶

(Bb approached through d minor)

p

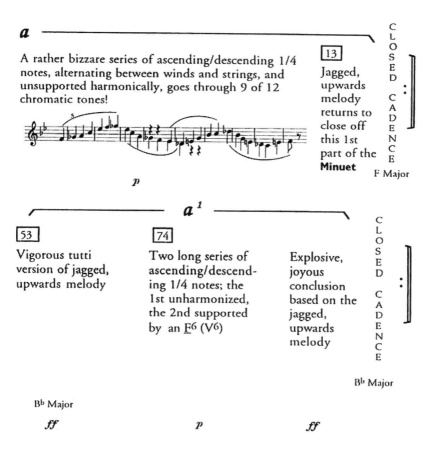

a

A rather bizzare series of ascending/descending 1/4 notes, alternating between winds and strings, and unsupported harmonically, goes through 9 of 12 chromatic tones!

p

[13]

Jagged, upwards melody returns to close off this 1st part of the **Minuet**

CLOSED CADENCE

F Major

a¹

[53]

Vigorous tutti version of jagged, upwards melody

Bᵇ Major

$f\!f$

[74]

Two long series of ascending/descending 1/4 notes; the 1st unharmonized, the 2nd supported by an F⁶ (V⁶)

p

Explosive, joyous conclusion based on the jagged, upwards melody

CLOSED CADENCE

Bᵇ Major

$f\!f$

"Un poco meno allegro (♩. = 88)"

Trio

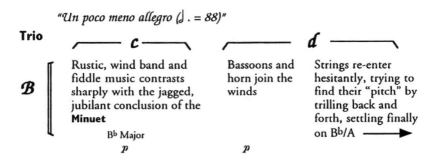

𝓑

⎡─── *c* ───⎤   ⎡─── *d* ───⎤

Rustic, wind band and fiddle music contrasts sharply with the jagged, jubilant conclusion of the **Minuet**

B♭ Major

p

Bassoons and horn join the winds

p

Strings re-enter hesitantly, trying to find their "pitch" by trilling back and forth, settling finally on B♭/A ⟶

Minuet

𝓐¹   Tempo I (This *da capo* is the same as **𝓐**, without the repeats)

‖ *a* ‖ *b* *a¹* ‖

Trio (as before)

𝓑 ‖ *c* ‖ *d* *c¹* ‖

Minuet/ <u>Coda</u>   (" *a¹* " portion of **𝓐**)

𝓐²

⎡ 180

Vigorous tutti version of jagged, upwards melody

ff

<u>Two</u> long series of ascending/descending 1/4 notes; the 1st unharmonized, the 2nd supported by an F⁶ (V⁶) harmony

p

200

The trio that follows is delightfully whimsical, a tongue-in-cheek gesture towards the old-style minuet with a country band of wind-players interrupted by a bunch of self-taught violinists who can neither hit the note in the middle nor control their bows adequately. How else can one sensibly interpret passages such as this?

The first notes are clearly 'wrong' while the *sforzando* is uncalled for.

— A. Hopkins

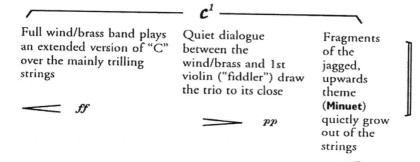

c¹

Full wind/brass band plays an extended version of "C" over the mainly trilling strings

ff

Quiet dialogue between the wind/brass and 1st violin ("fiddler") draw the trio to its close

pp

Fragments of the jagged, upwards theme (**Minuet**) quietly grow out of the strings

205

Explosive, joyous conclusion based on the jagged, upwards melody

MOVEMENT IV   *Sonata-Allegro form*

"Allegro ma non troppo (♩ = 80)"   duple meter (2/4)

Exposition

Theme 1

The theme is not so much a
"melody" as it is two brief motives,
which will be endlessly manipulated
to create the basic fabric of the music:

Part 1: 1st violins
hurridly play
fragment
illustrated at left,
giving way to
lower strings
which suddenly...

Bb Major

p

... reach
a tutti
cadence
after but
2 1/2 ms
of music

f

| 25 |

Modulating Bridge
Brief, apreggiated
figures passed from
violins to winds

ff ▷

| 37 |

Theme 2
Tasty little village-band type
theme momentarily stops the
chattering 16th-note motion

oboe ➤ flute

a

F Major

p

(Note: Rolling triplet
accomp. in clarinet)

| 45 |

A somewhat
comic contrast:
the little Theme
is heard in the
low strings

cellos/ ➤ violins
basses

a¹

p

| 88 |

Cadence Material

Part 1: Brief cadence "theme," based
on **Theme 2**, is bounced between:

high   lower
strings & strings

2x total

ff

| 96 |

Part 2: Fanfarish winds, brass,
and 1st violins ring out over
furiously chattering motives **a** and
b in the other strings

ff

Perpetual mobile: This exhilerating movement is written in the style of an opera buffa overture. Its giddy, lighthearted character is to a great degree the result of its unrelenting rhythmic momentum and chattering melody.

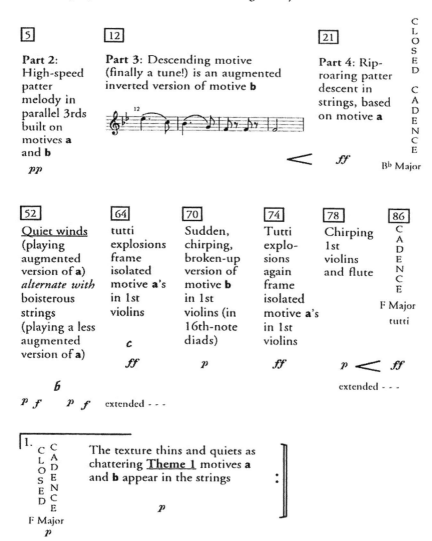

5

Part 2: High-speed patter melody in parallel 3rds built on motives **a** and **b**

pp

12

Part 3: Descending motive (finally a tune!) is an augmented inverted version of motive **b**

21

Part 4: Rip-roaring patter descent in strings, based on motive **a**

ff

Bb Major

CLOSED CADENCE

52

<u>Quiet winds</u> (playing augmented version of **a**) *alternate with* boisterous strings (playing a less augmented version of **a**)

b

p f   p f   extended - - -

64

tutti explosions frame isolated motive **a**'s in 1st violins

c

ff

70

Sudden, chirping, broken-up version of motive **b** in 1st violins (in 16th-note diads)

p

74

Tutti explo-sions again frame isolated motive **a**'s in 1st violins

ff

78

Chirping 1st violins and flute

p < *ff*

extended - - -

86

CADENCE

F Major

tutti

1.

CLOSED CADENCE

F Major
p

The texture thins and quiets as chattering <u>**Theme 1**</u> motives **a** and **b** appear in the strings

p

Development Full of good-natured energy and comic contrasts

100

Part 1:
C C
L A
O D
S E
E N
D C
 E

The texture thins and quiets
as chattering **Theme 1**
motives **a** and **b** appear in
the strings

F Major

p

p <

Tremolo
strings
join in

f <

<u>Big</u>, important
sounding octave "B"
in tutti would seem
to anticipate a <u>major</u>
event!
(B7 harmony implied to
E major/minor?)

149

Part 4: <u>Theme 1</u>
motives **a** and **b** in
1st violins under
sustained winds

pp <

(Like **Part 2** of
Cadence Material):
Fanfarish winds,
brass and low
strings ring out over
furiously chattering
motives **a** and **b** in
violins

Pedal "F"

ff

165

Part 5: Another big, serious
sounding moment would seem
to be upon us:
1) Explosive repeated chords and
descending F7(♭9) arpeggios over
syncopated "F" pedal
   alternates with
2) Sustained chords and isolated
motive as in middle strings

2x total

───────────────────────────────┤

ff

Recapitulation

189

<u>Theme 1</u> (abbreviated)
Part 1: Heard entirely in violins and viola (not
broken up between upper/lower strings as in
Exposition)
<u>Note</u>: Sudden tutti attacks shove the energy level up
another notch!

B♭ Major

f

Sudden tutti cadence
this time brings **Theme
1** to a premature
conclusion!

120

Part 2: Big event? E Major/
minor? Nah!
B♮ ◢ C (IV of G Major)
Strings and winds play
descending augmentation of **b**

winds   extended - - -

violins

low strings

131

Part 3: Varied, sparkling sequence
features:
1) Motive **a**'s bounced around strings
2) Rising/falling 3-note motives in
winds
3) Explosive 𝑓 𝑝 in low strings

<u>3x total</u>

1st x	2nd x	3rd x
g minor	B♭ Major	d minor

181

Part 6: Huh? The
energy dies away as
motive **a**'s echo
throughout the
strings

𝑝

184

In a devilishly difficult
little solo, a comic
sounding bassoon plays
<u>**Theme 1**</u> in anticipation
of the **Recapitulation** (or
is the bassoon lost? Overly
enthusiastic?!?)

𝑝

Low
strings
with
motives **a**
and **b**

193

Modulating Bridge (extended)
Brief arpeggiated figure is passed
from:

winds

winds

1st violins
𝑓

1st violins
𝑓

𝑝

strings
𝑝

Rip-roaring
cadence in
tutti

2nd violins
𝑓

𝑓𝑓 >

215

Theme 2

Little village band theme again appears over rolling triplet accompaniment in clarinet (2nd)

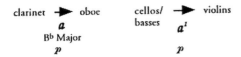

clarinet ➔ oboe   cellos/ ➔ violins
basses

a   *a¹*

Bb Major

p   *p*

230

Quiet winds (playing augmented version of **a** *alternate with* boisterous strings/flute (playing less augmented version of **a**)

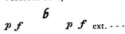

p f   *p f* ext. - - -

266

Cadence Material

Part 1: Brief cadence theme based on <u>Theme 2</u> is bounced between 1st violins and rest of strings

2x total

ff

274

Part 2: Fanfarish winds, brass and 1st violins ring out over furiously chattering motives **a** and **b** in lower strings

ff

Coda

278

Part 1: Much like Part 1 of the **Development**, suddenly quiet, upwards sequence of motives **a** and **b** in the strings

p ◁

327

Part 4:
1) Quiet winds in dialogue play an augmented version of **a**
2) Low strings play unaltered version of motive **a**!

pp

The strings manage one last burst of energy, entering with motives **a** and **b** against augmented winds

◁ *ff*

T
U
T
T
I   P
   A
   U
T   S
R   E
I
T
O
N
E

T
U
T
T
I   P
   A
   U
O   S
C   E
T
A
V
E

"F"

Bb/E (=C7)

      ©1998 The Teaching Company.

242				
Tutti explosions frame isolated motive **a**'s in violins	Chirping "broken-up" version of motive **b** in 2-note 16th units	Tutti explosions frame isolated motive **a**'s in violins	Chirping violins and flute	Tutti cadence in Bb Major
c				extended - - -
ff	*p*	*ff*	*p* < *ff*	

290		**298**	**300**	⌢	**319**
Syncopated, exclamatory chords in winds and brass	Quiet motive **a**'s in violins	<u>Theme 1</u> whispering version of theme, in 1st violins, clarinet and bassoon	Part 2: Huge cadential unit (explosive chords and furiously chattering strings) arrives on a	F7	Part 3: The "descending motive" (**Part 3** of <u>Theme 1</u>) appears in strings and winds over motives **a** and **b** in accomp. by overworked cellos and basses
f >		*pp*	*ff* > *p*		*pp*

Tired, worn out 1st violins play an augmented version of <u>Theme 1</u> ⌢	Exhausted bassoon plays a single motive **b** ⌢	Equally tired 2nd violins and violas answer the bassoon ("We're pooped, too!") ⌢	<u>Explosive Finale!</u> One last, herculean burst of energy brings the movement, and the symphony to a lively conclusion
Bb Major			
pp	*pp*	*pp*	*ff* *End of Symphony*

Timeline

1770 .... Beethoven is born in Bonn on December 17.

1789 .... Beethoven successfully petitions the elector of Bonn to grant the Beethoven brothers half their father's pension and to have their father removed from Bonn.

1792 .... Beethoven departs Bonn for Vienna, Austria, in November.

1796 .... Beethoven's hearing loss begins slowly.

1800 .... Symphony No. 1 is premiered on April 2.

1802 .... Beethoven writes the Heiligenstadt Testament in October.

1803 .... Symphony No. 2 is premiered on April 5.

1805 .... The "Eroica" Symphony is premiered on April 7.

1807 .... Symphony No. 4 is premiered on March 5.

1808 .... Symphonies Nos. 5 and 6 are premiered on December 22.

1809 .... Archduke Rudolph and Princes Lobkowitz and Kinsky sign contract of lifetime support for Beethoven.

1812 .... Beethoven breaks off his love affair with Antonie Brentano.

1813 .... Symphony No. 7 is premiered on December 8.

1814	Beethoven gives his last public performance as a pianist. He is enjoying a sudden increase in his popularity. Symphony No. 8 is premiered on February 4.
1815	Beethoven falls out of favor with the public. His hearing suffers another rapid deterioration. His patrons are leaving Vienna or are estranged from him. He is increasingly regarded as insane. His brother Caspar dies and he begins litigation to gain custody of his nephew Karl.
1824	Symphony No. 9 is premiered on May 7.
1827	Beethoven dies on March 26.

Glossary

Academy: Public concert in 18th century Vienna, Austria.

Arpeggio: Chord broken up into consecutively played notes.

Augmented:

1. Major or perfect interval extended by a semi-tone, e.g.: augmented sixth: C-A sharp.

2. Notes that are doubled in value, e.g.: a quarter note becomes a half note. Augmentation is a device for heightening the drama of a musical section by extenuating the note values of the melody.

Baroque: Sixteenth and 17th century artistic style characterized by extreme elaboration. In music the style was marked by the complex interplay of melodies, as manifest, for example, in a fugue.

Bridge: Musical passage linking one section or theme to another.

Cadence: Short harmonic formulas that close a musical section or movement. The commonest formula is dominant–tonic (V–I).

1. A closed (or perfect) cadence fully resolves: the dominant is followed by the expected tonic.

2. An open (or imperfect) cadence is a temporary point of rest, usually upon an unresolved dominant.

3. A deceptive (or interrupted) cadence is one in which the dominant resolves to some chord other than the expected tonic.

Cadenza: Passage for solo instrument in an orchestral work, usually a concerto, designed to showcase the player's skills.

Chromatic: Scale in which all the pitches are present. On a keyboard this translates as moving consecutively from white notes to black notes.

Classical: Designation given to works of art of the 17th and 18th centuries, characterized by clear lines and balanced form.

Coda: Section of music that brings a sonata-allegro movement to a close.

Crescendo: Getting louder.

Da capo: Back to the top, or beginning (instruction in a score).

Development: Section in a classical sonata-allegro movement where the main themes are developed.

Diminished: Minor or perfect interval that is reduced by one semi-tone, e.g.: minor seventh, C-B flat becomes diminished when the minor is reduced by one semi-tone to become C sharp-B flat. Diminished sevenths are extremely unstable harmonies that can lead in a variety of harmonic directions.

Dissonance: Unresolved and unstable interval or chord.

Dominant: Fifth note of a scale and the key of that note, e.g.: G is the dominant of C. The second theme in a classical sonata-allegro exposition first appears in the dominant.

Double fugue: Complex fugue with two subjects, or themes.

Drone: Note or notes, usually in the bass, sustained throughout a musical section or composition; characteristic of bagpipe music.

Dynamics: Degrees of loudness, e.g.: piano (quiet), forte (loud), indicated in a musical score.

Enharmonic: Notes that are identical in sound, but with different spellings, depending on the key context, e.g.: C sharp and D flat.

Enlightenment: Eighteenth century philosophical movement characterized by rationalism and positing that individuals are responsible for their own destinies and all men are born equal.

"Eroica": Soubriquet, literally meaning heroic, given to Beethoven's Symphony No. 3.

Exposition: Section in a classical sonata-allegro movement where the main themes are exposed, or introduced.

Fermata: Pause.

Forte: Loud.

French Overture: Invented by the French composer, Jean Baptiste Lully, court composer to King Louis XIV. The French Overture was played at the theater to welcome the king and to set the mood for the action on the stage. It is characterized by its grandiose themes, slow, stately tempo, dotted rhythms, and sweeping scales.

Fugato: Truncated fugue whose exposition is not followed by true development.

Fugue: Major, complex baroque musical form, distantly related to the round, in which a theme (or subject) is repeated at different pitch levels in succession and is developed by means of various contrapuntal techniques.

Gesamtkunstwerk: All-inclusive artwork or art form, containing music, drama, poetry, dance, etc.; term coined by Richard Wagner.

Heiligenstadt Testament: Confessional document penned by Beethoven at a time of extreme psychological crisis. In it he despairs over his realization that he is going deaf, but determines to soldier on.

Hemiola: Temporary use of a displaced accent to produce a feeling of changed meter. Beethoven uses it to effect an apparent change from triple (3/4) meter to duple (2/4) meter, without actually changing the meter.

Home key: Main key of a movement or composition.

Homophonic: A musical passage or piece in which there is one main melody and everything else is accompaniment.

Interval: Distance in pitch between two tones, e.g.: C-G (upwards) = a fifth.

Inversion: Loosely applied to indicate a reversal in direction, e.g.: a melody that goes up, goes down in inversion, and vice versa. Its strict definitions:

1. Harmonic inversion: The bottom note of an interval, or chord, is transferred to its higher octave, or its higher note is transferred to its lower octave, e.g.: C-E-G (played together) becomes E-G-C, or E-C-G.

2. Melodic inversion: An ascending interval (one note played after the other) is changed to its corresponding descending interval and vice versa, e.g.: C-D-E becomes C-B-A.

K. numbers: Koechel numbers, named after L. von Koechel, are a cataloging identification attached to works by Mozart.

Measure: Metric unit; space between two bar lines.

Melisma: Tightly wound, elaborate melodic line.

Meter: Rhythmic measure, e.g.: triple meter (3/4) in which there are three beats to the bar, or duple meter (2/4) in which there are two beats to the bar.

Metric modulation: Main beat remains the same while the rhythmic subdivisions change. This alters the meter without disturbing the tempo.

Minuet: Seventeenth and 18th century, graceful and dignified dance in moderately slow three-quarter time.

Minuet and Trio: Form of a movement (usually the third) in a classical symphony. The movement is in ternary (ABA) form with the first minuet repeated after the trio and each section itself repeated.

Modal ambiguity: Harmonic ambiguity, in which the main key is not clearly identified.

Mode: Major or minor key (in modern Western usage).

Modulation: Change from one key to another.

Motive: Short, musical phrase that can be used as a building block in compositional development.

Movement: Independent section within a larger work.

Musette:

1. Bagpipe common in Europe in the 17th and 18th centuries.

2. Piece of music in rustic style with a drone bass.

Musical form: Overall formulaic structure of a composition, e.g.: sonata form, and also the smaller divisions of the overall structure, such as the development section.

Ostinato: Motive that is repeated over and over again.

Overture: Music that precedes an opera or play.

Pedal note: Pitch sustained for a long period of time against which other changing material is played. A pedal harmony is a sustained chord serving the same purpose.

Piano: Soft or quiet.

Piano trio: Composition for piano, violin, and cello.

Pivot modulation: A tone common to two chords is used to effect a smooth change of key. For example, F sharp-A-C sharp (F sharp minor triad) and F-A-C (F major triad) have A in common. This note can serve as a pivot to swing the mode from F sharp minor to F major.

Pizzicato: Very short (plucked) notes.

Polyphony: Dominant compositional style of the pre-Classical Era, in which multiple melodies are played together (linear development), as opposed to one melody played with harmonic accompaniment.

Quartet:

    1. Ensemble of four instruments.

    2. Piece for four instruments.

Viennese classical style: Style that dominated European music in the late 18th century. It is characterized by clarity of melodies, harmonies, and rhythms and balanced, proportional musical structures.

Recapitulation: Section following the development in a sonata-allegro movement, in which the main themes return in their original form.

Recitative: Operatic convention in which the lines are half sung, half spoken.

Retrograde: Backwards.

Retrograde inversion: Backwards and upside down.

Ritardando: Gradually getting slower (abbreviation: ritard.).

Scherzo: "Joke"; name given by Beethoven and his successors to designate a whimsical, often witty, fast movement in triple time.

Semi-tone: Smallest interval in Western music; on the keyboard, the distance between a black note and a white note, and also B-C and E-F.

Sequence: Successive repetitions of a motive at different pitches. This is a compositional technique for extending melodic ideas.

Sonata-allegro form (also known as sonata form): Most important musical structure of the Classical Era. It is based on the concept of dramatic interaction between two contrasting themes and structured in four parts, sometimes with an introduction to the exposition or first part. The exposition introduces the main themes that will be developed in the development section. The themes return in the recapitulation section and the movement is closed with a coda.

Stringendo: Compressing time; getting faster.

String quartet:

1. Ensemble of four stringed instruments: two violins, viola, and cello.

2. Composition for such an ensemble.

Symphony: Large-scale instrumental composition for orchestra, containing several movements. The Viennese classical symphony usually had four movements.

Syncopation: Displacement of the expected accent from a strong beat to a weak beat, and vice versa.

Theme and Variations: Musical form in which a theme is introduced and then treated to a series of variations on some aspect of that theme.

Tonic: First note of the scale; main key of a composition or musical section.

Transition (or bridge): Musical passage linking two sections.

Triad: Chord consisting of three notes: the root, the third, and the fifth, e.g.: C-E-G, the triad of C major.

Trio:

1. Ensemble of three instruments.

2. Composition for three instruments.

3. Type of minuet, frequently rustic in nature and paired with a minuet to form a movement in a Classical Era symphony.

Triplet: Three notes occurring in the space of one beat.

Tutti: Whole orchestra plays together.

Voice: A pitch or register, commonly used to refer to the four melodic pitches: soprano, alto, tenor, and bass.

Biographical Notes

Brentano, Antonie (1780–1869). Wife of Franz Brentano. Antonie was the "immortal beloved," the great love of Beethoven's life.

Beethoven, Caspar Anton Carl (1774–1815). Beethoven's brother, who married Johanna Reiss. Beethoven would later claim custody of their son Karl.

Beethoven, Johann (1740?–'92). Beethoven's father, musician and teacher.

Beethoven, Maria Magdalena (1746–'87). Beethoven's mother.

Beethoven, Nikolaus Johann (1776–1848). Beethoven's brother; apothecary.

Kinsky, Prince Ferdinand (1781–1812). Co-donor of Beethoven's annuity.

Lichnowsky, Prince Karl (1756–1814). Major patron of Beethoven.

Lobkowitz, Prince Josef (1772–1816). Patron, admirer and co-donor of Beethoven's annuity; major figure in the Austro-Hungarian Empire.

Maezel, J.N. (1772–1838). Inventor of the metronome and other mechanical instruments. The battle symphony ("Wellington's Victory") was his idea.

Neefe, Christian (1748–'98). Composer who introduced Beethoven to the works of Johann Sebastian Bach.

Razoumovsky, Prince Andrei (1752–1836). Patron and friend of Beethoven. Razoumovsky was the Russian ambassador in Vienna and one of the wealthiest and most brilliant men in Europe.

Ries, Ferdinand (1784–1838). Pianist and composer. Ries was a student of Beethoven and later his friend. One of Beethoven's earliest biographers.

Rudolph, Archduke of Austria (1788–1832). Son of Leopold II. Rudolph was a student of Beethoven and one of the three donors of Beethoven's annuity.

Schindler, Anton (1795–1864). Violinist and conductor. Schindler was a devoted friend of Beethoven and an early biographer.

Spohr, Ludwig (1784–1859). Violinist, composer, and conductor. He wrote an autobiography that contains anecdotes about Beethoven.

Bibliography

General Musical Interest

Kerman, Joseph. *Listen*. Third Edition. Worth Publishers, Inc., 1980. A superb, non-technical general music appreciation book spanning the last 1500 years of Western music history.

II. The Classical Era

Heartz, Daniel. *Haydn, Mozart, and the Viennese School, 1740-1780*. New York: Norton, 1995. A detailed and essentially non-technical study of the Viennese classical Style.

Rosen, Charles. *The Classical Style—Haydn, Mozart, Beethoven*. New York: Norton, 1972. A dense and rather technical study, this book is the standard text on the compositional aspects and genres of the Classical Era.

III. Beethoven Biographies

Solomon, Maynard. *Beethoven*. Schirmer Books, 1977. Simply the essential book on Beethoven, a psychobiography of extraordinary insight and breadth.

Robbins, Landon, H.D. *Beethoven*. New York: Macmillan, 1975. A lavishly illustrated book consisting of letters, eyewitness accounts, and anecdotes about Beethoven, arranged chronologically.

Notes

Notes